MARTIN CLASSICAL LECTURES

VOLUME XXVIII

The Martin Classical Lectures are delivered annually at Oberlin College on a foundation established by his many friends in honor of Charles Beebe Martin, for forty-five years a teacher of classical literature and classical art in Oberlin.

HERODOTEAN NARRATIVE AND DISCOURSE

MABEL L. LANG

Published for Oberlin College by
Harvard University Press
Cambridge, Massachusetts
and London, England
1984

Library of Congress Cataloging in Publication Data

Lang, Mabel L., 1917–
   Herodotean narrative and discourse.

   (Martin classical lectures; v. 28)
   Bibliography: p.
   Includes indexes.
   1. Herodotus—Style. 2. Narration (Rhetoric).
3. Oral tradition. I. Oberlin College. II. Title.
III. Series.
PA25.M3   vol. 28   937s [938'.03]   83–18436
[PA4004]
ISBN 0–674–38985–9 (alk. paper)

To Richmond Lattimore

Preface

The invitation to deliver the Martin Classical Lectures at Oberlin in 1982 was an honor that I wanted to share with Herodotus, since in all this distinguished series the Father of History has had no place since Charles Beebe Martin's inaugural lecture in 1929. I am sorry that Herodotus could not participate as well in the splendid hospitality and universal kindness with which I met. He would have written a *logos*, giving full marks to Oberlin's flora, fauna, customs, and history, but I can only express my gratitude to the community as a whole and special thanks to Professor Nathan Greenberg and Professor Susan Kane.

Even though Herodotus took the whole known world for his province, he managed to give his researches both focus and unity. My attempt, on the other hand, to deal with little more than Herodotus' nine books has resulted in disunity and diffusion. My excuse must be that the effort to demonstrate composition of an "oral" type almost requires a scattershot approach that aims at a variety of stylistic features, most of which cannot be followed up here in detail.

Discourse as a component of oral composition was the starting point of this study, but it ramified in an undisciplined fashion and in two opposite ways. Since speeches so often provided motivation and explanation of actions, they seemed to serve as connections between events. So from a macrostylistic point of view consideration of speeches led to the whole subject of narrative transitions. But the same speeches viewed microstylistically showed many oral characteristics, three of which seemed suitable for sample analysis: rhetorical questions, alternative, and proverbial expressions. The whole thus is a partial, piecemeal, and preliminary exploration of oral techniques in Herodotus' *Histories*.

The lectures appear here in the form in which they were delivered, but some supporting material has been added in the form of notes. More extensive documentation appears in the four appendixes, and indexes of Herodotean speeches and passages from both Herodotus and Homer serve as easy means of reference to the whole.

Contents

HERODOTEAN NARRATIVE
AND DISCOURSE

Conventions Used in Summaries of Speeches

Dealing with the great mass of Herodotean discourse (in Chapter 2 and Appendixes II and III) by means of quotation in Greek and/or translation would have been cumbersome in the extreme and would have emphasized the particulars of the individual speeches and dialogues rather than their patterned nature and structure. By summarizing the gist of each speech it was possible in brief compass to relate it to its context, whether narrative or dialogue, and to show basic formulas operating in a variety of situations.

The difference between directly and indirectly quoted speeches is indicated as follows: "X said: . . ." for direct quotation; "X said that . . ." for indirect. The tenor of a speech is indicated by the following abbreviations: Q, question; A, answer; C, challenge; R, response; S, synthesis or conclusion; I, information. An upper case letter indicates that the speech is directly quoted; lower case, that it is indirectly quoted. A letter enclosed in parentheses indicates that the speech is reported as having been made but is not indirectly quoted. Other conventions and abbreviations used in categorizing and reporting speeches are most fully described at the beginning of the Index of Herodotean Speeches.

Chapter 1

Narrative Transitions

Almost any reader of Herodotus' *Histories* can be happily drawn along by the narrative flow without worrying much about where he is going. But every once in a while even the most casual reader will stop and ask, "How did we get from there to here?" The problem of the ways in which Herodotus' narrative moves has been much studied for the light it might shed on the order of composition and on Herodotus' own processes of thought.[1] But no effort has been made, I think, to look for illumination in modern examples of oral narrative that are close to the kind of material which constituted Herodotus' sources and by which his own narrative style must have been affected.

To enter the world of oral tradition and set the mood of oral narrative, it will be useful to introduce as a parable a worldwide folk motif that is frequent in North American Indian tales and also found in Siberia, Melanesia, and Bolivia: ascent to the sky by a chain of arrows.[2] A typical example is from a tale of the Quillayute, who lived near Puget Sound; I quote the beginning:

A man who was against the Creator put the Sun in his bag. He opened the bag a little bit toward the way he was going. He took the Sun up into heaven. All the people who were on the side of the Creator began to talk about how they could go up to heaven to get the Sun back to light the world.

Wren decided that they could make a bow and arrows and shoot a ladder to the sky. A stout man split half a hewed log to make the bow with. Then all the stout animals—Whale and Bear and Mountain Lion—and all the deep-sea animals got together to make the bow. They made it, and then they got Man-eating Shark to shoot an arrow up to the sky.

He was the first one to shoot. He couldn't see the arrow when it struck up above. It was too far away. All the people—the land animals, the sea animals, and the birds—tried to see where the arrow was stuck up above. Only Snail could see the arrow Man-eating Shark shot. He was the only one with a good enough eye. Then Snail shot his arrow into Shark's arrow. He shot several

times. Mountain Lion, Kingfisher, and Little Hawk—all with good eyes—
shot arrows end to end. Then everybody could see the ladder. Everybody
shot. The ladder reached from the sky to the ground.[3]

This motif parallels in a naive fashion one aspect of Herodotean narrative, that is, the storyteller's way of structuring his tale both for
himself and for his audience by providing from time to time what we
should call a topic sentence, which takes aim at a point further on in
the story and thus gives direction to the narrative. By this means,
both speaker and hearer know where they are going.

In the beginning of a narrative, as in this Quillayute tale, there may
often be a first statement of direction that aims not at the end but at
a midpoint of the tale: "All the people who were on the side of the
Creator began to talk about how they could go up to heaven to get the
Sun back to light the world."[4] Only after this has pointed the way can
a second statement of direction aim at a nearer point through which
and by means of which the narrative must begin to travel to the
midpoint: "Wren decided that they could make a bow and arrows and
shoot a ladder to the sky." The excerpt that I have quoted moves
through the near point in its last sentence: "The ladder reached from
the sky to the ground." The next near statement of direction follows,
still aimed at the tale's midpoint: "All the people climbed up the
ladder to capture the Sun." This carries through to the midpoint at
which, after various adventures, they capture the Sun; only then is
the final point signaled: "Then Eagle called a meeting of all the people." This introduces the etiologies consequent on the Sun's capture
and the popular decision to put the Sun where it now is. Here we
learn why Snail is now blind, why Eagle and Hawk have the sharpest
eyes, and what became of the people left in the sky.

Although this kind of structuring by direction-statement seems to
be characteristic of oral composition generally, this particular tale
provides very specific reinforcement. That is, the shooting of the first
arrow, at which successive arrows must be aimed in order to make a
ladder, neatly parallels the directional statement that sets a goal
toward which the subsequent narrative is aimed. Even the difference
between arrow and statement sharpens the point of the parallel, for
while the material chain of arrows can be put together only by shooting ever backward from the first arrow, the narration can move *forward* by means of successive directional signals, thus making it clear
that the winged word has a far greater power of staying aloft than the

feathered shaft. In this way a chain of subsidiary directional state-ments may propel the narrative forward to reach a stated goal, with each statement hooking on to the farther end of its predecessor and ending with another hook for its successor, like the chain of arrows but in reverse.

And what does all this have to do with Herodotus? I think that we may find that it provides an easier explanation for the way in which his narrative moves than the somewhat convoluted, self-conscious, and literary reasoning ordinarily invoked. Thus, it should be noted that the first statement of direction does not aim at the end of the *Histories* but at some vague midpoint: "The account of the researches of Herodotus of Halicarnassus is here set down so that the memory of the past may not be lost: of the astonishing achievements both of the Greeks and of the foreigners; and more particularly, of the way in which they came into conflict." Only the causes and background of the Persian Wars are thus signaled in the beginning. Directional state-ments for the events of the wars themselves and for the Greek vic-tories will come only after the midpoint has been reached: "The Athe-nians refused (to take back Hippias) and in refusing decided on open hostility to Persia . . . The sailing of this fleet was the beginning of trouble not only for Greece, but for other peoples as well" (v.96–97).

If we follow up the metaphor of the arrow-ladder, we may say that as the first arrow in the Quillayute tale was the resolve to capture the Sun, so Herodotus' first arrow aims at "the way in which they came into conflict." The flight of this arrow gives the long-distance direc-tion in which follow-up arrows are aimed in order to traverse the more immediate and intervening space. The possible mythical causes of conflict are evoked and then immediately disposed of in favor of the one man who served as middleman between Greeks and Persians.[5] This Croesus is himself an arrow shot out to serve as a mark at which the narrative can aim as it steps back into his origins in order to give both context and impetus for his role as intermediary.

At this point it may be useful to mix metaphors and think of the directional statement as a carrot by which the narrative is led in the desired direction—forward—by means of nearer and successive car-rots that beckon on the way to the one most distant. Thus the cause of the conflict as a long-distance carrot requires first a point of departure—that is, once the mythical episodes are cast aside, Croesus as the Janus-figure between East and West. Croesus then as near-distant carrot introduces Lydian prehistory. When the narrative has gone through his predecessors to Croesus, Herodotus uses the divine nemesis that was to overtake Croesus as the new carrot to guide the narrative through the loss of his heir,[6] then uses as the next carrot Croesus' determination to conquer the Persians, which brings in the testing of oracles, and so on.

Both arrow and carrot may serve as symbols of the way in which the narrative seems to be led forward, but perhaps another fanciful way of looking at the organization of the whole may give clearer definition. That is, just because it is possible to identify a skeleton of causation, it is not necessary or even desirable to believe, as Immerwahr for example does,[7] that the narrative was constructed in this way, that it was conceived first as a causally articulated skeleton and then fleshed out with narrative. Such purposive articulation is the very antithesis of the Herodotean run-on style (*lexis eiromene*), which is more in harmony with a developing kind of organization that might occur naturally through growth when the expansion of the narrative forced articulation. That is, the way in which the narrative moves is not within a preconceived structure of logic and causality but, as Herodotus' own word "path" suggests,[8] is very like putting one foot after the other toward some destination already glimpsed. And as one may in traversing a path stop to examine some wayside wonder or even turn off temporarily to explore a tangential byway that enhances the view of one's goal, so the Herodotean narrative invites digressions both for their own sakes and for corroboration or verisimilitude.[9]

Significant for this kind of narrative progression is the way in which even movement backward in time is made in a forward direction. We have already seen how the digression on Croesus' ancestors moves from Gyges as the first of the line to Alyattes, Croesus' immediate predecessor; so also in the account of the Persians Herodotus uses Cyrus' accession to power as the arrow to point the way before he begins with the earliest foundation of monarchy among the Medes and moves forward in time to the Median king whose throne Cyrus usurped. By tucking the forward-moving account of an event's background between its first mention and its presentation, the historian achieves the illusion of causation; the event seems to grow naturally from what precedes, whether or not there was a real and actual connection.[10] It is thus that the run-on style can deal with the result of researches into the back-reaching traditions of several different peoples. Here is no carefully calculated account that brings into chronological relation the early history of Lydia, Persia, and Greece. Rather, the movement is by association, from Croesus as the middleman between Greece and Persia, whose background history is given only when it becomes relevant and will help define his position and role, to his conqueror Cyrus and the Median history that only now has significance.

Let us then forget for a moment the kind of elaborated, consciously pre-ordered arrangement that scholars trained in proper historical methods have attempted to show in the work of this first and most Homeric of historians. Recognizing both the largely oral nature of Herodotus' sources and, as a result of his "lectures," the likely oral manner of his composition, let us examine ways in which an oral narrative style may have influenced the "history" (that is, historicity) of Herodotus' work. Immerwahr, on the one hand, found in the *Histories* various patterns of form that he took as expressions of Herodotus' thought,[11] thus divining purpose from result and assuming that implicit in the patterns are Herodotus' ideas of history and a logical overall plan.[12] A student of Homer and the techniques of oral composition, on the other hand, might see not the thought informing and effecting the presentation but inherited techniques of narrative style both producing the way in which the material was viewed and affecting the individual items and their interrelation.[13]

A quick survey of some techniques of oral composition already adumbrated will serve to introduce an analysis of their use in sample passages of the *Histories*. First there are the arrows or carrots or topic sentences that by giving direction and impetus make possible the inclusion of digressive material without causing either composer or audience to lose track.[14] Long-distance pointers are supplemented by a series of nearer-distance directional statements that renew the narrative impetus in its approach to the long-distance goal. And many of the cases of so-called ring-composition should perhaps better be seen as a kind of spiraling forward, since the wrap-up statement does more than echo the beginning statement; it very frequently builds on the first statement by using material from the digression to make a new directional statement, thus moving the narrative forward rather than coming back to the same place. An example in Book v (55–66) will illustrate. The beginning statement is "Aristagoras left Sparta and went to Athens which had been freed of her tyrants in the following way." After ten chapters of description the wrap-up statement is "Athens which had been great even formerly then when she was rid of her tyrants became greater." The end statement thus points the way for the continuing narrative, which reports Athenian growth.[15]

A second characteristic of oral composition correlates with the first. Digressions that feed into an event in the main narrative often come directly after a topic sentence signaling that event, since there the narrative tension is great enough to minimize the sense of interruption. This digressive material of a background nature, which can be included because the overall direction is so clearly signposted, is always narrated in a forward fashion so that it ends up abreast of the main narrative and helps along the illusion that the past effects the present. Such a background digression is introduced in Book viii (27–30) when the Thessalians, having joined the Persians, threaten the Phocians, and Herodotus sketches in the history of Phocian-Thessalian enmity that preceded and by his account produced and explained the Thessalian hostility. Another digression detailing early Sicilian history and the rise of Gelon (vii.153–156) comes between the departure of messengers to ask aid of Gelon and their arrival; by this means the reader is prepared for Gelon's high-handed methods, and the messengers' arrival through space at Syracuse coincides with the arrival through time of Gelon at the peak of his power.[16]

The fact that such background digressions respect the chronology by building up to the signaled point may, however, create false expectations and lead to misunderstanding in the case of digressions that are probative or illustrative. Such a digression as that in which Herodotus "proves" that Cleisthenes' reform of Athenian tribes was in imitation of his grandfather's action in Sicyon (v.67–68) presents no difficulties and is historically harmless because the chronology is clear and the reader can decide for himself whether *post hoc* is necessarily *propter hoc*. But another digression that proves or illustrates a point may range widely without particular regard for chronology, so that the relation between the digression's end and the return to the main narrative may be historically deceptive even though the transition as narrative appears most appropriate. This appearance shows that association plays so important a role in the oral style that when the probative digression comes to an item of proof that is relevant to the subject matter of the main narrative, then the transition is effected. The analogy here is with railroad tracks: probative digressions, having made their tangential circle, come around to the main line on a parallel track and jump over, while background digressions feed directly into the main line. Perhaps the most famous example of the probative digression is in Book vii (139–145): when Herodotus stops to give due praise to Athens for her part in the defeat of the Persians, he notes that the Athenians' credit was the greater in that they acted despite warnings from Delphi. The following digression, which describes the oracles and the Athenian reaction, ends with the Athenian decision to embark their whole force aboard their ships and face the invader along with the other Greeks who wished to join them. This decree then serves not only as culmination of the digression and justification of the praise but also as an apparent introduction to the immediately following account of the general Hellenic council at the Isthmus, suggesting both a chronological and a causal link between the Athenian decree and the council meeting. That neither linkage is factual seems likely from the presumptive lateness of the embarkation decree compared to the Isthmian council's contemporaneity with Xerxes' arrival at Sardis in Asia Minor (vii.145.2).[17] The association of decree and council makes a good narrative transition with the digression apparently spiraling forward to join the main account, but from a historical point of view it goes too fast and too far.[18]

A third characteristic of oral narrative is the way in which all digressions, even those that are more incidental and merely relevant than those giving background or proof, then to come where suspense is sufficient to keep the audience involved. Related to this is the creative and potentially antihistorical use of what may be called flat spaces, that is, intervals when the illusion of time passing is achieved by the insertion of filler material. Thus in Book i.81–84:

(Croesus) sent these to ask them to help as quickly as possible since he was being besieged. He sent both to his other allies and to Lacedaemon. But the Spartans happened at this time to be caught in a struggle with the Argives. (A long chapter then describes the struggle and a short chapter tells of the herald's arrival, their preparations to help, and the further news that Sardis had fallen, so that the return to the narrative can assume a lapse of some thirteen days.) Sardis was captured in the following way: on the fourteenth day of the siege Cyrus made proclamation . . .[19]

A fourth technique of oral narrative is the use of hooks to connect marginally related passages; this use ranges from the ubiquitous *men-de* linking of a fairly mechanical sort to the planting in an earlier passage of a person or place so that his or its later and crucial appearance does not require a distracting explanation. In iii.129 when Darius' injured foot has been badly mauled by Egyptian doctors, someone can recommend Democedes without explanation, since four chapters earlier Polycrates was reported to have taken Democedes with him to Oroites. And when Oroites had killed Polycrates, he held captive all his entourage except for the Samians, so that when Darius arranged for Oroites' liquidation and the transport of all his possessions to Susa, it could be assumed that Democedes was there ready to be called on.[20] Just as the oral composer uses topic sentences to keep both nearer and farther ends in view, so with his mental eye being fixed on a tale that looms ahead he almost unconsciously begins to set the scene and gather the persons who will take part. It is not that he consciously foresees that a mention in passing in chapter 125 will make it possible for him to narrate the healing of Darius' foot in chapters 129–130 without backtracking to how Democedes had gone with Polycrates to Oroites and was then transported to Susa. Rather, the signaling of the episode to come beckons on—to a rendezvous, as it were—not only the author himself and his audience but also those who are to take part in the episode.[21] Democedes' full biography, we might also observe, waits till he has achieved the cure and serves as a preface to his plot to get back to Italy by means of a Persian spying expedition.

The first part of Book iii will show how some of these techniques fit into the running narrative. The first sentence there displays a hook and two topic sentences, one pointing to the main subject to come and the other for immediate use: "This Amasis was the Egyptian against whom Cambyses the son of Cyrus made his expedition . . . ; the reason for the campaign was the following." Amasis is a hook from Book ii; the announcement of the expedition provides direction for the narrative through chapter 38, and the reason announces the contents of the first three chapters. Here the anecdotes outlining versions of Cambyses' motive are not told in backward, causative fashion. For the first anecdote such a method of telling would be: Cambyses campaigned because he was angered by Amasis because Amasis sent him a substitute princess because he, Amasis, knew that Cambyses would not make her a royal wife because Cambyses had asked for an Egyptian princess at the suggestion of an Egyptian eye doctor who wished to make difficulties for Amasis because he had sent him to Persia because Cyrus had asked for the best oculist in Egypt. No, that would leave both author and audience stranded in the past and out of touch with the expedition that had been signaled; so the narrative is forward-moving, starting with Cyrus' request for an oculist and ending with Cambyses' anger at discovering the deception, thus coming abreast of, and feeding into, the main narrative and the intent to campaign.

The near-distance topic sentence is renewed in chapter 4: "There was another matter, quite distinct, which helped to bring about the expedition." This introduces Phanes, whose story is also told in forward fashion in such a way that it motivates his advice to Cambyses to send to the Arabian king with a request for safe passage. The illusion of time passing in the interval while this request is being made is achieved by a two-chapter digression on the approaches to Egypt, the waterless condition of the Arabian desert, and how at a later time that problem was solved. This time-filler thus goes chronologically far beyond the time of the expedition into Herodotus' own time, but as with a Homeric simile it illuminates by comparison and contrast, giving both background and foreground for Cambyses' actual passage through the desert. The digression is rounded off with a return to Cambyses who has in the interval achieved a treaty with the Arabian king. Relevance again results in a chapter of digression that starts with the Arabian form of treaty-making and goes on to name their gods, but the narrative, undeterred by this anthropological aside, continues with the Arabian king's method of facilitating the Persian passage into Egypt.

To fill in the time while that passage was being achieved, the narrative leaps ahead to establish the whereabouts of the Egyptian host. This combination of time-filler and narrative change of place is very close to that in *Iliad* 3 where, when heralds are sent from the battlefield to fetch Priam, the narrative goes ahead of them to the city wall so that the Teichoskopia scene fills in the time of the heralds' slower approach and allows us to be with Priam as he receives them. So also here we are to be on the receiving end, and a new near-distance topic sentence signals this: "Psammenitus, son of Amasis, lay encamped at the Pelusian mouth of the Nile, awaiting Cambyses" (iii.10.1). The usual background digression to explain how Amasis had been succeeded by Psammenitus follows, with a note about Amasis' burial to serve as a hook to Cambyses' later desecration of the royal corpse (iii.16). And presumably since Psammenitus' reign was to be so short, its most notable event, rain in Thebes, is tucked into this same digression.

The account of the battle and its aftermath involves various anecdotes and some digressive material of the sort that such events attract to themselves,[22] but we must turn to the next near-distance topic sentence at the beginning of chapter 17: "After this Cambyses took counsel with himself and planned three expeditions. One was against the Carthaginians, another against the Ammonians, and a third against the long-lived Ethiopians." The way in which Herodotus deals with the three expeditions thus forecast neatly exemplifies oral techniques. The very listing of the three with only the third group of people provided with an adjective is reminiscent of many Homeric lines that list three heroes or places and give an adjective only to the third, at the formulaic end of the line. The treatment of the three also has folktale overtones in that one and two are summarily treated while the third is elaborated. First the three are listed again with the nature of the attempt to be made: Carthaginians by sea, Ammonians by land, and a spying expedition at first to the Ethiopians. Then since spying implies something to be inquired about, a digression is required about the Table of the Sun which will serve as a hook to the Fisheaters' later Ethiopian visit to the Table. While the Fisheaters who can act as spies are being sent for, the time is filled with a brief account of the abortive naval expedition against the Carthaginians. And as Cambyses gives the now-arrived spies instructions and gifts for the Ethiopians, there follows a short digression on them that has now become useful as the Fisheaters are about to meet them. A long dialogue between the Fisheaters and the Ethiopian king first supplies the bow that hooks on to Cambyses' later disposal of his brother and heir and dramatizes the difference between the noble savage and the greedy Persians, thus serving as both warning and motivation for Cambyses, who all unheeding hastens to march into Ethiopia. Thus any historical cause of the Ethiopian expedition is passed over for the sake of a narrative connection that will prefigure its disastrous end. But although Herodotus emphasizes the rashness of Cambyses' headlong rush, his narrative at the same time requires him to have Cambyses send off the land expedition against the Ammonians so that the account of the Ethiopian fiasco can fill in the time needed for that Ammonian expedition to arrive so that it can be accounted for next.

Thus of the three expeditions forecast, the last mentioned is the one that becomes the vehicle that carries the other two, with the following entwined order: Carthaginians, Ammonians, Ethiopians; Ethiopians, Carthaginians, Ethiopians; Ethiopians, Ammonians, Ethiopians; Ammonians.

As the aftermath of the failed expeditions comes Cambyses' murderous reaction to the Egyptian celebration over the appearance of Apis (17–29). This serves as a hook into the topic sentence for chapters 30–38, which provide conclusive evidence of his madness: "And now Cambyses, who even before had not been quite in his right mind, was forthwith, as the Egyptians say, smitten with madness for this crime." Although the following anecdotes that illustrate his madness show much evidence of oral style, they could have come to Herodotus already in that form, so it is only the interconnections that provide certain evidence of Herodotean oral techniques. One example is the way in which Prexaspes' cupbearer son is unnecessarily mentioned in chapter 34 as an example of his father's favored position at court, so that when in chapter 35 Cambyses uses the cupbearer as a target to demonstrate his prowess with the bow, the effect on Prexaspes needs no explanation. This is not literary foreshadowing but the storyteller's way of working up to his point, incidentally preparing his audience for an immediate appreciation of the denouement by a kind of back-casting from the point at which he is aiming.

The most striking use in Book iii of forward-spiraling is in chapters 39 and following: "While Cambyses was carrying on this war in Egypt, the Lacedaemonians likewise sent a force to Samos against Polycrates the son of Aeaces." The expedition of the Lacedaemonians does not take place till chapter 54, and the topic sentence is renewed in chapter 44 and again in chapter 47, as in each case the intervening chapters provide useful background material, always told in forward fashion so that, starting in the past, it comes up to the notice of that expedition. Thus, after the first topic sentence Polycrates' rise to power and the effect of his unvarying good fortune on his friend Amasis lead up to the first renewal: "It was with this Polycrates, so fortunate in every undertaking, that the Lacedaemonians now went to war" (44). Then the account of the banished Samian nobles who turned to the Lacedaemonians for help leads to the next renewal: "Then the Lacedaemonians made ready and set forth to the attack of Samos, from a motive of gratitude, if we may believe the Samians, because the Samians had once sent ships to their aid against the Messenians, but as the Spartans themselves say . . ." (47). This introduces another more or less historical reason for the Lacedaemonian assistance.

The account of the Lacedaemonian expedition is still further deferred so that more background material concerning Samian-Corinthian relations can be added. Here it seems that Herodotus has determined to use Samos, as he had used Lydia before, as a steppingstone from Persian to Greek history. His decision to use the Persian story as his main thread was in general very wise, since it gave him both core and continuity with extensions into the non-Persian world to sketch in the whole context. Its chief disadvantage was that, although it allowed a very large digression on the customs and nature of Egypt, it did not, because of the rarity of early Greek-Persian contacts, allow similarly extensive treatments of Greek background. But Samos' early dealings with both Persia and various Greek states made *its* history a possible vehicle for making connections and bringing in items of Greek history. The only difficulty was that the most important part of this Samian history overlapped the reigns of Cambyses and Darius. In order to keep to the main Persian thread, then, Herodotus had to break up his Samian story rather awkwardly and return to it in two later sections of this book. That he here excuses the length of this first section on the grounds of Samos' three great construction projects seems to me not a denial of the use of Samos as a steppingstone but a convenient way of introducing these wonders.

The story motivating Corinthian help in the expedition against Samos has its own complicated charm, but what is most interesting about it is the question of whether the connections here made represent historical causes or narrative convenience. Since there is no mention of Corinth in the subsequent account of the Lacedaemonian expedition against Samos, and since Herodotus' account of Corinthian-Samian hostility is contradicted by other sources,[23] it is possible that Corinthian motivation for, and even Corinthian participation in, the Lacedaemonian expedition are less fact than the kind of fiction that grows out of the narrative need to make connections and to contain a wide assortment of material in linear form.

This analysis of the first part of Book iii is perhaps a sufficient sample of the way Herodotus utilized certain oral techniques in making narrative transitions. That there are in addition other forms of transition is obvious; of these the one that seems most familiar to the modern reader is the temporal connection, indicating the contemporaneity or posteriority of events. But the means of transition that seems most familiar to the modern reader is the temporal connection, indicating the contemporaneity or posteriority of events. But the means of transition that seems to me most appropriate and likely to appeal to a researcher like Herodotus—one who asked, one who learned, one who heard, and one who saw—is the use of knowledge as an impetus to action. And it is true that a persistent feature of Herodotus' style is the use of a verb of learning, in participial form or in a subordinate clause, to effect a transition from one state or action to another. Such bridges have gone unnoticed and unremarked, presumably because of their apparent naturalness: A did or said something; B, learning of this, did or said another thing. These verbs of learning not only operate as narrative bridges but also, at the same time, seem to provide temporal connection with, and motivation for, the following action, and so give the impression that the learning is all. Such a bias seems natural for Herodotus, for whom inquiry and the learning that resulted were of the first importance. And in addition the problem of arranging all that he had learned and reducing it to linear narrative made easy transitions very attractive. We, however, are so in the habit of looking to history for both strict chronology and an account of causes that we may often be led into assuming that the easy transition is temporally accurate and a full-dress motivation as well.

In order to put the verbs of learning used as transitions into the context of Herodotus' own learning and so make the connection between knowledge evoking action in the narrative and knowledge affecting composition by the researcher, we should first sample instances where Herodotus speaks personally of his own learning or knowing.[24] The first example is certainly causal and gives motivation:

Knowing (*epistamenos*) that human happiness never continues long in one state, I shall discourse equally of both. (i.5.4)

He uses the same participle concessively in other places when he does not wish to write something that he nevertheless knows:

Although I know his name, I shall not mention it. (i.51.4)
I shall write in this way, although I know three other ways in which the story of Cyrus is told. (i.95.1)

Although I know the height to which the millet and sesame grow, I shall not make mention of it, since I am aware that what I have already said concerning the fruitfulness of Babylonia has met with much disbelief on the part of those who have never been there. (i.193.4)

Other examples using the verb *punthanomai* indicate merely an outside source for his knowledge, perhaps to relieve him of responsibility:

As I learned by inquiry, this temple is the oldest of all those dedicated to this goddess. (i.105.3)
When the Ionians were in distress . . . , I learn that Bias made a most useful recommendation to them. (i.170.1)
In my judgment this is their wisest custom, which the Illyrian Eneti also have, as I learn. (i.196.1)
This I judge to have been the fiercest of all the barbarians' battles; and this, as I learn, was the manner of it. (i.214.1)

One other instance in Book i uses the verb *oida* and explains it with the verb to hear (*akouo*), thus indicating one of the senses through which knowledge comes and which along with seeing may be used to motivate actions and thus achieve transitions:

So much I know, having heard it from the Delphians.[25] (i.20.1)

Herodotus' references to his own knowing or learning show that although he considers it important in itself and as a guarantee of sorts, he only rarely considers it a motivating factor. Hence it is not necessary when in his narrative someone acts having learned something to view the knowledge as causal rather than as simply transitional. Nor is the implied temporal relation necessarily immediate. And although both causal and temporal connection may often be present, neither is exclusive, but there is the possibility of both other causes and intervening events. In other words, just as Herodotus' references to his own knowing or learning are incidental and seem mostly to lend verisimilitude, so it is possible that his subjects' learning and knowing are similar and that his use of them as transitions is more a function of his narrative style than a declaration of historical causation.

More than fifty examples of this kind of transition occur in Book i. The verbs used most frequently are *punthanomai*,[26] *akouo*, and *manthano*, with a few examples of *horao*, *gignosko*, *oida*, and *epistamai* as well as periphrases like "it was reported that." A concentration of six examples within eleven lines (i. 96–97) illustrates some at least of the variety:

This Deioces desiring power acted as follows. Since the Medes then lived in villages, he, who had even before been distinguished in his own village, still more applied himself to the practice of justice. And he did this when there was much lawlessness throughout the land, *knowing* that injustice is an enemy to justice. The Medes from his village, *seeing* his actions, made him their judge. And he was honest and upright, since he desired the rule. And acting thus he won not a little praise from his fellow citizens, to such an extent that men from other villages *learning* that Deioces alone gave straight judgments and previously having suffered unjust decisions, then when they *heard* gladly came to Deioces for justice and finally went nowhere else. When those who came became ever more numerous, as they *learned* that his judgments accorded with fact, Deioces, *knowing* that everything now depended on himself, refused to sit in judgment.

First, Deioces "*knowing* that injustice is an enemy to justice" seems to be causal, giving motivation similar to Herodotus' motivation for including both great and small cities, but there is a difference. Herodotus knew his own motivation, but in Deioces' case he apparently had to deal with a despot who was supposed to have gained what amounted to unjust power by the exercise of strict justice. Here the knowledge motivates only the means of making himself indispensable, and the contradiction between means and end provides ironic commentary. This kind of explanation, which anticipates or forestalls questions or objections, seems to be a regular feature of oral style,[27] and Herodotus often imputes knowledge of some relevant sort to his actors in order to explain what might otherwise appear to be un-motivated action. Thus a motive is provided that both eases narrative transition and satisfies audience curiosity; only as historical causation does it leave something to be desired.

In "The Medes from his village, *seeing* his actions, made him their judge," the participle is both causal and temporal. It is a perfectly natural transition and neatly exemplifies our maxim that not only must justice be done, it must be seen to be done. Then the use of both the learn-by-inquiry verb and the verb "to hear" motivating the men from other villages to come to Deioces for judgments shows the story-teller's instinct for suggesting a picture: that is, men of neighboring villages asking where justice could be obtained and thus hearing of Deioces. Finally, Deioces "*knowing* that everything depended on him" is probably more temporal than causal, implying that he waited to spring his trap till he was sure of his power.

These examples show the way in which narrative flows, as characters are activated by learning, and as successive accessions of knowledge ties the action together. But it may be objected that in this case we have Herodotus presenting practically unchanged the storytelling tradition as it came to him, and so it is not his style that we are examining. In order to test this, we should turn to one of the later, more "historical" books and to a passage less likely to be a traditional story:

> (In summary) Megabazus leads the Persians against the Paeonians; the Paeonians, *hearing* that the Persians were coming, march to the sea to ward them off; the Persians, *hearing* that the Paeonians were guarding the coast, turned inland and fell upon the Paeonian cities; when the Paeonians *heard* that their cities were taken, they dispersed and gave themselves up. (v.15)

Each action is tied to the previous one in the most natural manner: A acts; B learns of A's action and acts; A learns of B's action and reacts; B learns of A's reaction and responds. Is not this perfectly natural sequence exactly the way things happen? Perhaps, but life is not ordinarily so neat and tidy. For instance, it seems odd that in the wilds of Paeonia it should have been possible for the Persians, who needed guides, to have got more immediate information about the Paeonians' whereabouts than the Paeonians could obtain about the invaders. And yet if it had happened that the Paeonians had simply surrendered, this is the best story they could have invented. Here again, on this supposition, Herodotus would have been simply recounting what he was told, and although his own narrative style was bound to be affected by the style of his sources, it is difficult to be sure what he himself contributed. Perhaps a fairer test will be to examine all the uses of *punthanomai*, for example, in a section of one of the more historical books to see what part narrative-transition-by-learning plays in the overall organization of events.

> The Phoenician fleet sailed against Ionia. The Ionians, learning this, sent counselors to Panionion. (vi.7.1.)
> The Ionians provided various numbers of ships. The Persian generals, having learned these, were afraid. (vi.9.1)
> The Samians took Zancle while the Zancleans were out on campaign. The Zancleans, when they heard, came to the rescue. (vi.23.3)

News came to Histiaeus at Thasos that the Phoenicians were sailing against Ionia; having learned this he left Thasos. (vi.28.1)

They killed Histiaeus and sent his head to Darius, who, having learned of their action and condemning it, ordered that the head be buried. (vi.30.1–2)

The Lampsacenes captured Miltiades. Croesus, having heard, ordered them to release him. (vi.37.1)

Miltiades arrived and kept to the house, manifestly out of respect for his dead brother. The chiefs roundabout, hearing this, gathered to pay respects. (vi.39)

In these thirty-nine chapters of Book vi the verb *manthano* is also used six times in the same way to make a transition from one action to another. There seems to be no doubt, then, that transition-by-knowledge is a Herodotean device and not merely that of his sources.

The importance of what one learns as a possible cause of action as well as a linking device is confirmed in a variety of situations where failure to act on some piece of information is seen to be a mistake:

If having learned this Cambyses had changed his mind and led his army back, he would have shown himself wise after his original mistake. But paying no attention he kept going forward. (iii.25.5)

The Pythian priestess did say this much, that vengeance would come for the Heracleidae on the fifth descendant of Gyges. Neither the Lydians nor their kings paid any attention to this prophecy until it was fulfilled. (i.13.2)

When these words (Tomyris' threat if her son was not returned to her) were reported to him, Cyrus paid no attention, and Tomyris' son . . . killed himself. (i.213.1)

So great is the importance of the word as accompaniment of the wonderful deeds Herodotus had set out to record that not only does reported information serve to connect actions but the effectiveness of speech is frequently demonstrated as Herodotus' actors address one another directly. Throughout the work both dialogues and isolated speeches serve to clarify, to interpret, to justify, and to motivate attitudes as well as actions. And it is the various ways and apparent patterns in which speeches of this sort function as kinetic factors in the narrative that will be the subject of the next chapter, as we continue to study the extent to which Herodotus' style makes his history and how it affects his historicity.

Chapter 2

Patterns of Discourse

"In order that the things done of men not be obliterated by time," Herodotus the Father of History made inquiry his object and people his subject. And since his only way of preserving the memory of human achievements and events was by "replaying" them in words, the results of Herodotus' *historia* or research had to be presented in narrative. For although representations in painting and sculpture might have been possible, they had neither the range nor the efficiency that cinematography would one day be capable of. And although dramatic replay was both possible and attempted, ancient dramatists for the most part avoided the actual and factual in favor of the mythical since drama was properly concerned, as Aristotle first observed, with universals that could be created in poetry rather than with particulars that could be discovered by research. Drama, despite its literal meaning of "doing" or "action," was far more concerned with speaking and passion.

Still, a kind of static representation of the past was possible through narrative if not only the "what" and the "who" could be determined by inquiry but also, to provide context, the "where" and the "when." For these four aspects of his work Herodotus' predecessors in logography had shown how to string names and places on geographical and chronological or genealogical threads, so when his narrative dealt with these matters he could follow those masters. If, however, the narrative was to move from event to event, from person to person, from place to place, and from time to time, it was necessary for Herodotus to inquire also into the "why" and the "how" to provide motive force. And the masters to whom he could look for models in dealing with the answers to these questions must have been the epic poets and tellers of tales. Only through the influence of these traditions was it possible for a narrative describing people, events, times, and places to take on the life and immediacy of a reenactment as it gave speech to the actors to illuminate the "why" and the "how" of their actions.[1]

Thus the complete record had to include both deeds and words, but the difference between reported action and reproduced speech created an effect comparable to that of a play in which the actors are seen only as shadows but the voices are real. Deeds related in words could not have the same reality or vitality as words presented as words. To illustrate how different such reporting and reproducing are in kind and effect, we may take a part of a Herodotean speech and compare it with the way in which it would be presented if it were reported as an action:

> The Athenian messengers said: ". . . Having agreed with us to oppose the invader in Boeotia, you played the traitor and allowed him to invade Attica. For this the Athenians are angry with you, for you have not acted as you should . . ."
> The Athenian messengers reproached the Spartans with their failure to keep their agreement to join in opposing the invader in Boeotia.
> (ix.7)

Direct speech is thus seen to play a vital and important role in Herodotus' *Histories*. Not only is it different in nature and effect from narrative, there is also a difference in the kind and degree of authority or evidence that Herodotus had for the two. Since it is generally agreed that his inquiries were most often made of people and his sources were most often oral, it is probable from what we know of oral tradition that the combination of speech and narrative was already present in his raw material. But that versions of events undoubtedly came to Herodotus already complete with dialogue need not mean that the speeches he presented were in all respects the same as those he learned. One reason for assuming that he accorded the *erga* and *logoi* of his oral sources different treatment is that although he frequently gives variant versions of an event or action, he nowhere suggests that there was any question about the form or substance of a speech.[2] Since nothing seems less likely than that there was exact agreement as to the dialogue in versions retailed to him by several sources, we must assume that he regarded the words of his actors differently from their deeds. And since the consistency that has often been noted in the points of view and morality expressed by his speakers in very different times, places, and circumstances is difficult to square with the necessarily great variety of sources, we should assume that some, at least, of the uniformity of sentiment was supplied by Herodotus, the one person who dealt with all of the material. That this is a reasonable assumption is shown by the way in which Herodotus used speeches and dialogues not only to dramatize confrontations and interrelationships but also to explain why and how actions were initiated. For example, a man was persuaded to a course of action by means of a speech that had both the "historical" function of providing external motivation for the action (why he was impelled so to act) and the "rhetorical" function of showing what kinds of argument and forms of persuasion were effective (how he was influenced to act).[3] And it is because of the consistency of the views expressed in such speeches that the work is characterized by what is often referred to as Herodotus' philosophy of history or, more pejoratively, his moral bias.

Although discourse, reported both directly and indirectly, plays a large part in the *Histories* of Herodotus, it has received comparatively little attention.[4] Historians have discounted the conversations and single utterances as too obviously unhistorical to merit much serious consideration. Literary critics, on the other hand, have found the stories that are thus dramatized too slight and artless to be worthy of stylistic investigation. But now that both historians and philosophers of history are concerned with the way in which the appearance of historical causation is affected by the very process and form of narration,[5] it is time to look to the Father of History for light on the way in which oral traditions were first transformed into historical narrative. And since that historical narrative is studded with scenes in which the actors speak their own lines, analysis of that discourse's nature and function is important for an understanding of both Herodotus' historical techniques and his historical materials.

A survey of Herodotean discourse will not only demonstrate its quantity and quality but also give some indication both of ways in which it is used and of its historical effect. The numbers are impressive. In addition to many indirectly quoted single utterances and pairs in which both speeches are indirectly quoted,[6] there are 92 directly quoted single speeches and 164 dialogues made up variously of directly and indirectly quoted speeches: 59 pairs, 26 triads, 47 tetrads, 16 pentads, 9 hexads, 3 heptads, and 1 each of octad, ennead, decad, and decahexad.[7]

The single speech is one that stands alone and neither responds to anything spoken, directly or indirectly quoted, nor evokes a spoken reply, quoted directly or indirectly. It springs, as it were, full-armed from the action and seems to exist more purely for its effect on the action and the action's effect on it than for its own sake, as sometimes seems to be the case with those dialogues that constitute little scenes apart from the action. The single speech ordinarily involves a command, appeal, advice, or announcement, and like most other Herodotean discourse it has three chief functions: motivating, explaining, prefiguring. Most frequently it motivates, as when the Medes come together and say, "Let us have a king" (i.97.3); or when one Scythian urges the others, "Do not dignify these slaves with arms; get out your whips" (iv.3.3–4); or when Miltiades tells Callimachus, "It is up to you to decide whether Greece shall be slave or free" (vi.109.3–6); or when the Megarians at Plataea say, "We cannot hold out any longer by ourselves; come help" (ix.21.2). Secondly, single speeches may explain a situation or demonstrate an attitude like Xerxes' reproach to the Hellespont as he had it fettered and flogged (vii.35.2) or like Cambyses' unsuccessful appeal to the Persian nobles to avenge the usurpation of his throne, the only effect of which is an explanation of his situation (iii.65). Finally, single speeches may warn of coming trouble and be unheeded so that a disaster is both prefigured and justified: thus Sandanis' advice to Croesus against war with Persia warns of the defeat for which Croesus becomes responsible by ignoring the warning (i.71.2–4).[8]

In addition to single speeches that are isolated in the narrative, there are speeches in some dialogues that not only are separable from the pairs, triads, tetrads, and so on with which they are combined but are in every other way like these independent singles. Some fifty-eight such dependent singles occur as introductions or conclusions to the various pattern dialogues, providing impetus either for the following speeches or for the resulting action.[9] Of course, it might be said that all dialogues are basically made up of nothing other than single speeches, but in pairs, at least, many of the speeches are different from singles by their very relation to each other. That is, in order to fulfill the pair's function, which differs from that of the single speech, each half needs either to be evoked or to be answered. Question-and-answer speech pairs introduce or accompany situations that require a two-step approach, so that the advice or information which motivates or explains can only be evoked by a question; thus only in answer to Cyrus' question as to where the Lydian troubles will end can Croesus suggest a solution that motivates Cyrus' action (i.155). Or it takes a challenge-and-response pair to provide both motivation and preparation for the way the subsequent action turns out, as when Croesus' appeal to Adrastus motivates Adrastus' escort of his son on the boar hunt, but Adrastus' answer that a man dogged by misfortune has no place in sporting expeditions is needed to prepare for his fatal spearthrow that kills the boy (i.41–42). The two speeches of a pair are also needed for prefiguring if a situation involves not just a warning unheeded but a positive command or appeal that must be explicitly rejected, as when the Greek herald's appeal to Xerxes for recompense for Leonidas' death is rejected as Xerxes turns the appeal over to Mardonius, thus providing ironic explanation and justification of Mardonius' subsequent payment with his life (viii.114).[10]

Pairs and single speeches of these sorts are not only more numerous and ubiquitous in Herodotus' *Histories* than any of the longer dialogues, but they are the raw materials, as it were, out of which the longer dialogues are composed.[11] Thus the thesis-antithesis-synthesis pattern of the triad employs a pair and a single, or it may be made up of two overlapping pairs that combine the question-answer pattern with the announcement-response pattern in such a way that the second speech becomes both answer and announcement. The most usual tetrad pattern simply joins together two complete pairs, while pentads may be made up of triad plus pair or single plus tetrad, and so on for the longer dialogues. Being made up, then, of single speeches and pairs, these triads, tetrads, and so on share with their components the same general functions of motivating, explaining, and prefiguring, but obviously as wholes they are not only greater than the sum of their parts but also must multiply the effects of those parts. We must look therefore to see how they differ in function and situation from the independent singles and pairs.

Triads, unlike pairs and single speeches, which are the stuff of everyday life, have a kind of artificiality that makes it worthwhile to look at epic precedents for possible patterns of format and use. Of the twenty-seven triads in *Iliad* 1–12, ten are made up of a question-answer pair followed by a single that comments variously on the answers.[12] Two examples show how the triad adds a new dimension to both motivating and explaining: Diomedes asks, Who are you? Glaucus answers that he is grandson of Bellerophon; Diomedes concludes that as paternal guest-friends they must not fight (6.123). Apollo asks, Shall we stop the fighting for today? Athena answers Yes, but how? Apollo suggests that Hector challenge some Achaean to a duel (7.24). Without the build-up of the pair the third speech would appear abrupt and unmotivated; with the build-up it is possible to introduce in the third speech material that is strictly unnecessary but very helpful in enhancing the overall effect.

Each of the other seventeen triads in *Iliad* 1–12 uses a challenge-response pair of one kind or another followed by a single speech that draws a conclusion or synthesizes the two.[13] Here particularly the second speech is seen to be Janus-headed, so that it not only counters the first but evokes a response and so serves as a pivot of two overlapping pairs. Examples with only two speakers (*aba*) show the way in which a position taken by the first speaker in accord with the narrative line can be modified by means of the second speech so that the narrative may be given a new direction.

Agamemnon: I fear that I have caused your death.
Menelaus: The wound is not mortal; do not fear for me.
Agamemnon: I hope you are right; a doctor will help.
(4.155)

Athena: You are not the man your father was.
Diomedes: I was only following your orders.
Athena: No longer need you avoid gods; go after Ares.
(5.800)

Triads with three speakers come even closer to a thesis-antithesis-synthesis pattern, since the third speaker either compromises or chooses between the two positions taken by the first and second speakers.

Agamemnon: You avoid battle as your father never did.
Sthenelus: You lie; we are better men than our fathers.
Diomedes: Hush, it is his duty to spur us on.
(4.370)

Antenor: Let us give back Helen and her possessions.
Paris: I will not give her up; the possessions may go.
Priam: Let us propose that and also a truce for burial.
(7.348)

How do Herodotus' twenty-six triads compare? Seventeen are made up of a question-answer pair followed by a concluding sentence. As in the Homeric examples, the build-up here makes possible either change of direction or inclusion of unnecessary but relevant material.

Cyrus asked whether the feast or the day of toil was preferable.
Persians said the difference was great, between all good and all bad.
Cyrus: Revolt with me and you shall have all these goods and many more.
(i.126.3–6)

Xerxes asked if it was possible for the river to reach the sea by another channel.
Guides: This is the only exit.
Xerxes: The Thessalians are wise to surrender knowing how easily their country could be flooded.
(vii.128–130)

The other nine Herodotean triads use a challenge-response pair, as for example:

Otanes: Monarchy is bad; democracy is good.
Megabyzus: Democracy is as bad as monarchy; aristocracy is good.
Darius: Neither democracy nor aristocracy can be as good as monarchy.
(iii.80–82)

Spartans: Help us to restore Hippias as tyrant in Athens.
Corinthian: We can not support despotism, since it produces terrible results.
Hippias predicted that Corinth would regret leaving Athens free.
(v.91–93)

In both the *Iliad* and the *Histories* the triadic dialogue has much the same make-up and is used for similar purposes: a pair building to a conclusion that gives new impetus to the narrative either by change of direction or by embellishment. As simple motivation is the most frequent function of single speeches, and as pairs deal most often with situations needing explanation, so their combination in triads unites both functions to provide not only a commentary on the action but also an interpretation of the considerations important to the people involved.

The chief tetrad pattern presents a completely different picture. It is the doubled pair which through a two-stage challenge and response not only narrows the focus of attention by degrees but also for that very reason seems to be characteristic of an oral style. That is, a listening audience's attention and comprehension can best be nursed

along by small advances and explicit modulation, and the oral narrator must himself provide what in a literary work might be read
between the lines. He must do this both for his own sake in order to
maintain a tight hold on his narrative thread and for the purpose of
keeping his audience constantly involved. Obviously it is not possible
to say that the use of this two-stage pattern is limited to oral style
since this, like many characteristically oral motifs, themes, and techniques, persists by virtue of familiarity and habituation in literary
style as well; the difference is in the regularity and hence apparent
necessity of its use in oral narrative as opposed to the occasional and
casual use in written literature.

That Homer was not unacquainted with the two-stage challenge
and response and was even on occasion constrained by its pattern is
suggested both by the fact that eight of the ten tetrads in *Iliad* 1–12
have this format and because one of them uses it despite awkwardness.[14] In 1.352 ff. Achilles appeals to his mother for compensation
from Zeus for the dishonor done him by Agamemnon; Thetis accepts
his appeal by urging him to tell all; Achilles then expands on the
original appeal with background information, explicit definition of
the honor requested, and recommendations as to how it is to be done;
Thetis accepts. Homer seems to have been at the mercy of the two-
stage pattern, since he was compelled to motivate the reappeal by
having Thetis claim an ignorance that the poet then has to make
Achilles question in order to save divine credit for omniscience. Compare two other examples:

Aeneas: See if you cannot shoot Diomedes.
Pandarus: I have tried but only wounded him in the shoulder.
Aeneas: Join me in my chariot and let one of us take him on.
Pandarus: You drive, then, and I will try him with my spear.
(5.171)

Agamemnon: I will give her up, but find me another prize.
Achilles: There is no common stock; wait till we take Troy.
Agamemnon: I will have another prize even if I have to take yours.
Achilles: You do not appreciate me; I shall go home.
(1.106)

In all these cases, the first pair of speeches initiates a confrontation
that is given emphasis and enlargement by the second pair. There are
only two speakers in each case, so that the two pairs do indeed
represent a kind of softening-up process, or what sportswriters would

call a "one-two" attack. Thus by presenting the substance of challenge and response in two stages, the poet has achieved a cumulative effect and has more than doubled his audience's involvement.

Although the constituent pairs themselves of such two-stage tetrads are in many respects the same as independent pairs, they do differ in that neither pair is complete in itself. The reason for this seems to be that what is asked for or challenged in such a tetrad is complex rather than simple, and it requires either this two-stage treatment or a single pair in which the question or challenge would not be simple and immediate but would involve a speculative leap into the future. Thus in Book 1 Agamemnon would have to foresee that an objection would be made to finding a new prize and so make his threat to take the prize of someone else along with his demand. That kind of complication and foresight, although frequent enough in literature, seems foreign to oral composition from the point of view of both composer and audience, whose control and understanding are facilitated by single-track narration. Therefore, situations that require tetrads made up of two-stage pairs are likely to be those where the question or challenge is complex.

The purest and simplest examples of the two-stage challenge-and-response pattern in Herodotus' *Histories* are those involving a request for information followed by an answer that is sufficiently obscure, incomplete, unsatisfactory, or wrong to evoke a second and different question. The dialogue between Croesus and Solon (an octad made up of two tetrads) illustrates this twice over, as it sets the tone for the *Histories* as a whole both thematically and technically:

Q1 Who is happiest?
A1 Tellus.
Q2 How?
A2 Explanation.

q3 Who is next?
A3 Cleobis and Biton, with explanation.
Q4 Do you scorn my happiness?
A4 Explanation: man is all accident.
    (i.30–32)

It is easy to see in the first pair of the second tetrad that Herodotus can have Solon answer the "Who?" question with both name and explanation, so that the two stages of the first tetrad are more a matter of style than lack of skill. The first tetrad is simple, with the first short answer provoking a request for elaboration. Then, just as the second pair of that tetrad builds on the first pair, so the second tetrad builds on the first tetrad with a first pair that covers the same ground as the whole first set, leaving the second pair to bring king and poet-philosopher into direct confrontation and to point the moral of the whole dialogue. In the first tetrad the second question is motivated by the obscurity of the first answer; in the second tetrad the second question is evoked by the unsatisfactory (from Croesus' point of view) answer to the first question.

In eight of the independent two-stage tetrads it is the obscurity of the first answer that evokes the second question or challenge. Samples are:

q1 Spartans ask what god they should invoke to defeat Tegea.
a1 Oracle says that they should bring home Orestes' bones.
q2 Spartans ask location of bones.
A2 Oracle: Where there is blow on blow.
    (i.67)

Q1 Darius: Which relative do you wish to save?
A1 Intaphernes' wife: My brother.
Q2 Darius: Why brother rather than husband or sons?
A2 Intaphernes' wife: I cannot get another.
    (iii.119.3–6)

Other second-stage question-and-answer pairs result from dissatisfaction with the answer to the first question, as was the case with Agamemnon's reaction to Achilles' objection and with Croesus' reaction to Solon's naming of the second happiest men in his second tetrad. Dissatisfaction with such a "wrong" answer is most often expressed by a more forceful repetition of the question, which is made either more pointed by threats or more explicit by added detail. When the first pair is challenge and response rather than question and answer, the unsatisfactory response is a rejection of the challenge, which may be in the form of a command, reproach, or appeal, so that the repeated challenge brings to bear new arguments that speak to the objection made in the first refusal. Samples of the ten tetrads that exemplify this pattern are:

q1 Astyages asks where he got the boy.
a1 Mitradates says he begot him.

c2   Astyages says he is not wise thus to ask for trouble.
r2   Mitradates tells the true story.
    (i.116.3–5)

c1   Samians make a long appeal.
r1   Spartans say they do not understand.
c2   Samians show the sack and say it lacks meal.
r2   Spartans say the sack is superfluous.
    (iii.46)

C1   Cleisthenes: You have danced a wife away.
R1   Hippocleides: Hippocleides does not care.
C2   Cleisthenes: I award my daughter to Megacles.
r2   Megacles says yes.
    (vi.129–130)

Only in this last example are there three speakers in a two-stage tetrad, necessitated by the irremediably unsatisfactory response to the first reproach. The very exceptional use of a third speaker in what is so definitely a two-person pattern points up Hippocleides' exclusion.

A third group of these tetrads is characterized by the incompleteness or inadequacy of the first response that evokes a second question or challenge adding a new dimension. That is, the first answer is only part of the needed knowledge, mostly because the question was too limited, being simple rather than complex; or the first challenge was accepted but did not extend far enough. Samples of the eleven such are:

C1   Atossa: You should be adding to the empire.
R1   Darius: I know and am planning an expedition to Scythia.
C2   Atossa: Scythia can wait; I want some Greek slaves.
R2   Darius: All right, I shall send a spying expedition.
    (iii.134)

q1   Spartans ask who and whence they are.
a1   They say they are Minyans from Lemnos.
q2   Spartans ask what they want.
a2   Minyans say they want a share in the land.
    (iv.145)

Generally speaking, a two-stage dialogue can double the effect achievable in a single exchange, since the repeated give-and-take or cut-and thrust increases the dramatic impact and gives both more importance to the ideas and sentiments expressed and more personality to the speakers than a single pair of speeches. But the more immediate and obvious function of two-stage dialogues, like that of many single exchanges, is to answer questions of why and how. Sometimes these questions are large and historically or ideologically important, as in the case of the Croesus-Solon dialogue, which not only prepares the ground for Croesus' downfall by showing his heedlessness of advice but also asserts the importance of deferring judgment to the end. Herodotus seems here to be making explicit one of his primary principles of historical interpretation: to judge after the end is to judge by result, and only by the result or outcome can otherwise unknowable intentions and postures be divined and evaluated. Throughout the *Histories* Herodotus' knowledge of ends seems to influence his judgment of beginnings. One simple example is the way in which only undertakings that turn out badly are preceded by warnings, the disregard of which appears both to explain and to justify the result, just as here Croesus' disregard of Solon's warning precedes his downfall and makes possible his *pathei mathos*.[15]

In a similar fashion, a two-stage dialogue between Xerxes and Demaratus points up the contrast between Persian and Greek ideology and thereby explains both how and why the Greeks will be victorious.

q1 Xerxes asks what the Spartans are doing.
A1 Demaratus: They are preparing to fight.
q2 Xerxes asks how so few will face so many.
A2 Demaratus: Treat me as a liar if it is not so.
    (vii.209)

Since the Greek superiority is more spiritual than material, no narrative account could convey the power of that spirit so effectively as an expression of personal, firsthand conviction, especially when that is provoked by and contrasted with the incredulous challenges of the invading hordes' absolute master. Again the answers to questions and provocation serve not only to make explicit basic forces shaping the course of events but also to prepare the ground for a great king's failure by showing his disregard of warnings.

Most of the two-stage tetrads have less wide-ranging significance and answer more specific questions of why and how. Several seem to have as their sole purpose the eliciting of information necessary as background for subsequent action[16] or conclusions,[17] the uncovering of a motive for a particular act,[18] or a combination of both.[19] It is as if Herodotus was concerned to forestall inquiry and objection by presenting action as the natural outcome of a realistic exchange between his principal and an appropriate informant or instigator. It has always been assumed, indeed, that Herodotean dialogues were more realistic than real, and the present effort is to show that their realistic nature results not from free and unfettered invention in each case but from their patterned, typical quality rendered acceptable by close imitation of the actually real. Just as in popular tales of all sorts there are formulas of phrase and theme to ease transitions and motivate actions, so in the popular tradition that Herodotus both used and exemplified the pattern of two-stage question and answer may be invoked to account for new or changed directions in the course of events.[20]

A second kind of tetrad has as parallel in the *Iliad* only 1.59, where Achilles' challenge to some prophet to interpret Apollo's anger is answered by Calchas' challenge to Achilles to protect him if he does so; then Achilles' response to Calchas' challenge is followed by Calchas' interpretation of Apollo's anger, that is, his response to Achilles' challenge. This tetrad may be called chiastic since the correspondence of pairs is between extremes and means, so that the first question or challenge evokes a second question or challenge, the response to which makes possible the response to the first question or challenge. Examples from the *Histories* are:

q1	Eleans asked if they could arrange things better in the Olympian games.
q2	Egyptians asked if their own citizens took part in the contests.
a1 (to q2)	Eleans said they did.
a2 (to q1)	Egyptians said they erred and in justice should exclude them. (ii.160)

Q1	Someone: Do you see that Artemisia has sunk an enemy ship?
q2	Xerxes asked if it was truly Artemisia who had done it.
a1 (to q2)	They said it was, for they recognized her ensign.
A1 (to Q1)	Xerxes: Apparently my men are women, my women men. (viii.88)

The fourth speech is a comment acknowledging and answering the first question, but it is made only after Xerxes has asked the wrong question and received the right answer. He should have verified that the sunken ship was an enemy, not that Artemisia was the agent. This kind of irony delighted the Greeks.

All of the chiastic pairs seem to be fairly independent anecdotes in which the final response most often has a gnomic quality or an element of surprise that points a moral.[21] The other nine independent tetrads are made up of two more or less loosely connected pairs and show no effect of patterning.[22]

Most pentads in the *Histories* may be analyzed into pair and triad or single and tetrad (or tetrad and single), but the difficulty in most cases of deciding which pattern is dominant indicates that the whole has an existence and value over and above those of its component parts. An example illustrates:

Pair: Cyrus: Ask whatever you want.
Croesus: Let me reproach the god.
Triad: Cyrus asks why he wants to do that.
Croesus explains how the oracle deceived him.
Cyrus: You may do this and anything else you wish.
(i.90)[23]

As in the case of other pentads, it might be possible to justify classifying the first four speeches as a tetrad, but the consequent isolation of the last speech is difficult to reconcile with its strongly "synthetic" character. But it is this very wedding of the pair-triad with tetrad-single that makes the pentad a pattern in its own right. Compare the following:

Pair: Spako asks why Harpagus sent for him.
Mitradates: To make me expose this child.
Triad: Spako begs him not to expose the child.
Mitradates says he is unable otherwise to evade the inspector.
Spako: I just had a dead child; exhibit it and raise the live one.
(i.111–112)[24]

Pair: Aristagoras: Save the Ionians from Persian slavery and win much wealth.
Cleomenes: I defer my answer till the day after tomorrow.
Triad: Cleomenes asks how far from the sea it is to Persia.
Aristagoras says it is three months' journey.
Cleomenes: Go! You are asking the impossible.
(v.49–50)

There is an oddity here: Cleomenes' first response seems neither to be motivated nor sufficiently important to be reported in direct discourse. It is almost as if the pair-triad pattern forced Cleomenes to finish off the pair with a noncommittal response so that his final reaction could come as the result of a question and answer.

Pair: Persian asks what city he is from.
Thersander says he is an Orchomenian.
Triad: Persian: I warn you that few of all these Persians will survive.
Thersander: Should you not tell this to Mardonius?
Persian: What must be must be, for no one will believe.
(ix.16)

The separation in thought here between the pair and the triad is evident. Indeed, there seems to be very little point in the question-and-answer pair at all, since it is not even sufficiently epic to include a request for Thersander's name. And since every couch had a Persian and a Greek and since the Persian was speaking Greek, he could not merely have been making sure that Thersander was not Persian. It almost seems that there was a need felt for some introduction to the triad, not only for the sake of courtesy but also to fill out a pattern. Certainly the last speech is sufficiently gnomic to qualify as a punchline!

These pair-triad pentads, which can also be viewed as tetrads capped with punch-lines, all make good anecdotes. They do not for the most part motivate action so much as explain how it came about, for example, that Croesus taxed Delphi with deception, that the child Cyrus was saved by a shepherd, and that the Spartans did not assist in the Ionian Revolt. The anecdotes are strong on characterization as well, since for Herodotus, as for oral tradition, it is personalities who make history.

Does this Herodotean pentad pattern have a precedent in epic? Of the three five-speech dialogues in *Iliad* 1–12, two present the same kind of conflation of pair-triad and tetrad-single with two pairs followed by a solution; one of these two[25] explains how it came about that the Trojans broke the truce:

Pair: Zeus: Shall we stir up war again or bring peace?
Hera: Peace would nullify all my efforts.
Triad: Zeus: All right, you may destroy Troy, but someday I shall take one of yours.
Hera: You may do so, but now let us start up the war.
Zeus (to Athena): Go arrange that the Trojans break the truce.
(4.7)

Other pentads in the *Histories* are too various to be presented briefly,[26] so we shall do well to complete our survey of the longer dialogues. Six of the nine hexads in the *Histories* are made up of three pairs; they function either as a three-stage parallel to our two-stage tetrads or as a combination of unified tetrad and separable pair. Obviously the three-stage pairs go one step further than the two-stage pairs and are useful in situations that require as background a more extended exchange of information or opinion than the two stages permit. A simple example in indirect discourse will illustrate:

Pair: Darius asks where the girl is from.
          The Paeonian brothers say she is Paeonian.
Pair: Darius asks who the Paeonians are, where they live, and why they
          came to Sardis.
          The brothers give the identity and location of the Paeonians and say
          they have come to join him.
Pair: Darius asks if all their women are so industrious.
          The brothers say yes.
          (v.13)

The three pairs build in linear fashion, taking one step at a time, although the compound second question shows that it is not the difficulty of asking more than one question at a time that produces this kind of build-up.[27] The motivation for Darius' transplantation of the Paeonians is made clear only in the final pair, but the previous questions provide a background that lends both verisimilitude and an epic flavor to the exchange.

Hexads in general, including the tetrad-pair combinations and the three others with two triads or single and pentad, seem to have no function peculiar to the form that is not shared to some extent with other dialogues, but they do have room, by reason of their length, to develop a theme or clarify issues better than many of the shorter dialogues. In consequence, even when the hexad is used to motivate an action or explain a situation, it can provide as well both characterization of the individuals involved and the rationale of their positions. This is certainly the case with one epic hexad that may well have helped to establish the pattern:

Pair: Odysseus: Agamemnon offers gifts if you return to battle.
          Achilles: He dishonored me; let him suffer.

Pair: Phoenix: Better to return now with gifts than like Meleager to come
         later without.
         Achilles: I have honor enough from Zeus; but stay here with me.
Pair: Aias: Achilles has no care for his comrades; we do urge you to soften
         your heart.
         Achilles: I am still angry but when the Trojans come to my ships then
         I shall fight.
         (9.225)

Achilles' gradual progression from stiff-necked refusal to concession
is portrayed through the cumulative and various appeals made by the
three who challenge him; all are characterized thereby, and the issues
are clarified.[28]

Although much might be said individually of the seven dialogues
longer than hexads, evidence of patterning in them is largely limited
to their component parts. Thus the three heptads differ in make-up as
follows: pentad and pair (i.88–89); tetrad and triad (i.158–159); single
and hexad (iii.61–63). The division in each case is based on similarities between the component parts and independent dialogues of
the same length. The one octad (i.30–32) we have already seen is a
combination of two two-stage tetrads.[29] The only ennead (v.18–19) is
made up of a tetrad, pair, and triad; despite interspersed action both
between and within the parts, it operates as a unified whole.[30]

Perhaps the most impressive and most patterned dialogues in the
whole work are the decad of Book vii (46–52) and the decahexad of
Book iii (21–23), for very different reasons. All ten speeches of the
decad are quoted directly and fall neatly into three patterns: triad,
pentad, pair.

Triad: Artabanus: Your change from self-congratulation to weeping is odd.
         Xerxes: All this splendor will be gone in a hundred years' time.
         Artabanus: Sadder still is the certainty of troubles in our brief span.

In this first triad Artabanus' curiosity evokes an answer based on
appearances to which Artabanus reacts with a reminder of grim realities, thereby establishing himself as Xerxes' spiritual adviser and
warning him of the uncertainty of life and the instability of fortune.

Pentad
Pair: Xerxes: Without the dream would you have continued to try to pre-
         vent this expedition?
         Artabanus: I am still afraid, thinking that the two mightiest forces are
         against you.

Triad: Xerxes: What two? Are my army and navy not sufficient?
Artabanus: Not these, but sea and land are not sufficient for army and navy.
Xerxes: No need to borrow trouble; nothing ventured, nothing gained.

Xerxes thus shakes off Artabanus' warning as he takes his turn to question, both showing his heedlessness and linking the pentad to the preceding triad. This pentad is made up of a pair and a triad, but, as happens so often with such pentads, the question and answer of the triad also combine with the question and answer of the pair to make a two-stage tetrad. That is, the second question attempts to dispel the obscurity of the first answer in order to allow both speakers to present their positions in a step-by-step fashion. In these pairs Artabanus' responses present particular dangers that give body to the theoretical perils of the human condition that he outlined in the first triad, but in the final speech of the pentad Xerxes again brushes these aside with a lecture on manifest destiny and the need to act. Thus, Xerxes' conclusion here answers Artabanus' conclusion in the first triad, setting activist against passivist, or optimist against pessimist, or a fool rushing in against an angel fearing to tread.

Pair: Artabanus: Even so, do not trust the Ionians to fight against their cousins.
Xerxes: Do not worry; they were loyal before in Scythia, and we have hostages.

This final pair mirrors the first triad in coming back to the particular situation: Xerxes' easy and superficial pessimism has gradually been converted to an equally easy and superficial optimism in the face of Artabanus' very real pessimism, so that when Artabanus warns him against using the Ionians he brushes aside this warning also. By means of the reversal of Xerxes' mood and the contrast between Xerxes and Artabanus, Herodotus has been able both to portray Xerxes as the overconfident aggressor who is heedless of warnings and to present the hazards in his situation that will result in his failure. The whole dialogue thus brilliantly illustrates the way in which confrontations confirm and strengthen positions rather than change them.

Something of the same end-to-end correspondence of both form and content may be seen in the largely indirect exchange between the Fisheaters and the Ethiopian king in Book iii.[31] The sixteen short speeches contribute to a cumulative effect; the point being made is not complex, as in the Xerxes-Artabanus dialogue, but is rather a simple one that is compounded with examples and thus illustrates the extent of dialogue-patterning even more than do the complex examples.

Pair: Fisheaters: Cambyses sent us to have converse with you and he gives these gifts.

         King: He does not want friendship but unjustly covets this land. Tell him to thank god that we do not desire his land.

Triad: King asked how the garment was made.

         Fisheaters described the dye process.

         King said that Persians were as deceitful as their garments.

Triad: King asked about the the gold jewelry.

         Fisheaters described its use as necklaces, etc.

         King said that the Ethiopians had stronger chains.

Triad: King asked about the myrrh.

         Fisheaters described its use.

         King said the same as about the garments.

Triad: King asked what Persians ate and how long they lived.

         Fisheaters said they ate bread made from grain and lived at most 80 years.

         King said they would not live so long on such a diet except for the wine; in this alone they bested the Ethiopians.

Pair: Fisheaters asked about the Ethiopian diet and life-span.

         King said many lived 120 years and they ate boiled meat and milk.

The pairs at beginning and end frame four triads; the first pair, in direct discourse, sets the general tone of the confrontation between Cambyses' spies and the virtuous Ethiopians. This is made more specific in the triads about the gifts. The last pair echoes the first in that the Fisheaters take the initiative by asking a question that both underlines the Ethiopian superiority adumbrated in the first pair and serves as motivation to begin the actual spying part of the Fisheaters' mission when their wonder about longevity takes them to the light-water spring.[32]

     This survey has intended to show the extent and nature of dialogue-patterning in the *Histories*. From the structural point of view that patterning seems to me a characteristic of the oral style. As far as content is concerned, the next two chapters will sample some of the ways in which the oral style is evidenced within the speeches.

Chapter 3
How Could Herodotus Imitate Homer?

Five different ways of asking the question in my title may illustrate both the difference between information-seeking questions and rhetorical questions and at least some of the varieties of rhetorical questions. *How* could Herodotus imitate Homer? asks for information about the ways in which imitation might be effected. How *could* Herodotus imitate Homer? seems to be rhetorical in its implication of absurdity—that imitation of Homer was the last thing any self-respecting historian would consider. How could *Herodotus* imitate Homer? is probably rhetorical in its suggestion that Herodotus of all people was least likely to do this. How could Herodotus *imitate* Homer? might be asking for information but is more likely to be suggesting that what he really does is controvert Homer. And finally, How could Herodotus imitate *Homer?* rhetorically underlines the absurdity of the historian's being influenced by the poet.

My title is supposed to be not only provocative and illustrative but also indicative of what I want to discuss, that is, a comparison of Homer and Herodotus as presumed oral stylists, with regard to their use of the question as a literary, rhetorical, and even historical device. Without more ado we can dispose of simple question-and-answer pairs that elicit information; these are used in similar fashion by Homer and Herodotus (and most others as well) both to dramatize personal interaction and to introduce relevant material in a natural and realistic fashion. Thus Priam's questions to Helen about the Greek warriors in *Iliad* 3 (162–242) not only motivate characterizing descriptions for the benefit of both Trojans and epic audience but also point up Helen's situation and relationship with the Trojans. Similarly, in Herodotus' *Histories* Croesus' questions to Solon (i.30–

32) about the happiest man not only evoke characterizations of happiness but also dramatize the confrontation between king and poet-philosopher.

Different from the questions that expect an answer and whose primary function is to evoke that answer are the questions asked to show that they are unanswerable. These constitute one variety of the so-called rhetorical question—that is, a question asked for effect rather than for an answer.[1] Rhetorical questions may also serve to capture attention, to challenge the audience, and sometimes to prepare the ground by opening closed doors, as it were, for persuasion by the speaker in his own answer to the question. A Homeric question may illustrate: Achilles asks Agamemnon, "How will the Achaians give you a prize? (1.123). The question not only challenges Agamemnon's assumption that he should be recompensed for the loss of Chryseis and shows up the absurdity of his demand by its unanswerability but also motivates Achilles' own explanation of how impossible is the redivision of once-divided spoil.

If we find parallels in the use of such rhetorical questions between Homer and Herodotus, we may or may not suspect influence, depending on our individual attitudes to a *post-hoc-propter-hoc* view of causation. It may of course be that a certain sameness of the human condition makes for a certain similarity in the use of a tool so handy and effective in discourse of all kinds. Differences in the use will be both more interesting and more open to interpretation, since the differences of time, genre, subject matter, and purpose between Homer and Herodotus must be taken into account.

Perhaps the most remarkable difference may be seen in the use of questions that are asked by the narrator himself. Homer's questions of this sort are all very much the same: "Who of the gods brought them together in strife?" (1.8); "Then whom first, whom last did Hector slay?" (5.703);[2] and "How then could Hector have escaped death if Apollo had not for the last time stood close by him?" (22.202). It is presumably the Muses who are being asked, so that these questions are an alternative for the command to the Muses to tell all, as in the introduction of the Catalogue of Ships,[3] but it is the poet who provides the answer and so demonstrates the rhetorical nature of the question. Although the invocations to the Muses seem to lend a higher authority to what follows, the poet's use of the question with his own answer has as its chief function the focusing of attention on new material or a change in the direction of the narrative. One other question is asked, not so much to motivate an answer as to relieve the poet of responsibility: Homer asks (17.260), "Who of men could tell the names of all the rest who roused the Achaians to battle?" Here, too, it is presumably the Muses who are credited with complete knowledge, as in the introduction of the Catalogue.

Herodotus' use of rhetorical questions in his own person is more frequent, more varied, and more complex than Homer's. Of the ten examples in the *Histories*, five show Herodotus asking a question as it were of an opponent, and the questions are of the kind described by an ancient rhetorician as *to eis atopon apagein*[4]—that is, *reductio ad absurdum*.

(The Halys River was reportedly divided into two streams so that the Lydian army could cross it.) Some say that the old stream was completely dried up, but this I do not accept, for how could they have crossed the (completely diverted) river when they returned? (i.75.6)

The Ionians maintain that only the Delta is Egypt . . . But the Delta, as the Egyptians themselves say, and I agree, is a comparatively recent alluvial deposit. If then their land did not exist, why did the Egyptians make such a business of thinking they were the first men? (ii.15.1–2)

The third view (of why the Nile floods its banks) is most false . . . maintaining that the Nile runs from melted snow . . . how indeed could it run from snow, coming as it does from the hottest places to colder? (ii.22.1–2)

The Greeks in saying this (that the Egyptians sacrificed Heracles) seem to me to be completely ignorant of Egyptian culture. For if it is not holy for them to sacrifice animals except sheep, bulls, calves, . . . and geese, how could they sacrifice men? (ii.45.2)

(The Dodonean priestesses told about a black dove that flew up to them from Egypt and spoke to them in a human voice. Herodotus' opinion is that a woman came speaking a foreign language and presently, having learned Greek, spoke understandably.) As long as she spoke in a foreign tongue she seemed to them to utter bird noises, for in what way could a dove use human speech? (ii.55–57.2)

In each of these cases Herodotus presents the view of an authority with whom he disagrees and then neatly demolishes it with a question that reveals its illogicality. This use of the rhetorical question might be called the argument from improbability. Unlike Homer's own questions, which seem to invoke the authority of the Muses, these actually question authority and introduce an element of debate.

It is uncertain, however, whether the difference in use and function between Homer and Herodotus is more the result of developing rhetorical technique or more a reflection of the difference between traditional narrative style and critical modes of research. The other five questions that Herodotus himself asks are quite different from the first five in that the question is asked not of an authority with an opposing view but of the possibly skeptical audience. Some of these questions are more argumentative than others, but all seem designed to convert to a point of view. Their phrasing as questions instead of as simple declarations is presumably to arouse interest and, in the words on one handbook on rhetoric,[5] to take "the reader into partnership with the writer, as it were, in conducting the investigation."

(Herodotus asserts his belief that the Nile valley was originally a long, narrow gulf of the sea, comparable to the Arabian Gulf.) If the Nile should wish to turn its stream into this Arabian Gulf, what would prevent its being filled up by the stream within 20,000 years? Actually, I expect it would be less than 10,000 years. How then would not a gulf even far bigger than this one (that is, the Nile valley) have been filled by so great and so active a river in the length of time before my birth? (ii.11)

The reader is swept along by means of the questions to which he can give only the answers the argument requires and is thereby convinced of the Nile's land-making powers to an extent unlikely if they had been simply asserted.

A similar question justifies Scythian invincibility:

(The Scythians alone have an unfailing formula for self-preservation.) For being a people without cities or walls, horse-archers who get their living not from the plough but from cattle and have their houses on wagons, how could they not be invincible and impossible to come to grips with? (iv.46.3)

Unlike the previous specifically disputatious questions, these involve an argument from probability rather than improbability. In the next example that probability is made explicit.

(An inscription on the pyramid was said to record 1,600 silver talents as the amount expended on radishes, onions, and leeks for the workmen.) If this is so, how much else is likely to have been spent both on the iron with which they worked and on the food and clothing for the workers? (ii.125.6–7)

Somewhat different are the questions Herodotus asks to convey the size of the Persian expedition against Greece:

(Various mythical and early historical expeditions are listed.) All these armies and others in addition are not the equal of this one. For what people did Xerxes not lead out of Asia to Greece? What stream was not drunk dry except for the large rivers? (vii.21.1)

These questions are concerned not with pointing up probability but with providing evidence for Herodotus' assertions about the vast size of Xerxes' expedition. Again the question form arouses interest and perhaps disarms objections in a way that forthright declaration would not.

Still another kind of question is asked in order to focus attention on the answer that follows. Although like the preceding examples it does involve audience participation, it also brings us full circle to the Homeric questions that provide narrative transitions:

From all over Greece and also from Phoenicia jars full of wine come into Egypt every year, and yet not one empty wine jar, so to speak, is to be seen there. Where then, one might ask, are they piled up? I shall explain this too . . . (And he proceeds to do so.) (iii.6)

With this exception, however, the difference noted before between Homeric and Herodotean questions remains the same, and more and more we are tempted to assume that the two suggested causes are part and parcel of each other. That is, as in the passage of time questioning became more detailed, more acute, and more profound, it turned into inquiry or *historia;* and as interest turned from a world-view based on myth and traditions of an elusive past to the realities of the present, questions of how, why, what, and when became more searching. So large a generalization about the origin of both natural philosophy and history in the context of questions asked by Homer and Herodotus surely deserves itself to be questioned. Why are we tempted to see in these questions, which are the small change of ordinary communication, a clue to the development of larger movements and cultural advances? I suppose it is because these questions are such a natural and unconscious part of their environment that they can serve as symptoms or tiny outward manifestations of more basic attitudes and so, as they show changes in form and content, reflect changes in those basic views. So just as Plato shows Socrates convincing Ion that the epic poet is inspired by the divinity rather than possessed of skill and knowledge, so Homer's questions invoke the Muse while Herodotus skillfully uses questions in a spirit of scientific inquiry whereby partial knowledge can be made to increase understanding of the whole.

Although the differences between the questions asked by Homer and Herodotus might thus be seen as reflections of their different ways of attaining truth (Homer's by inspiration and Herodotus' by investigation), examination of the questions which both put in the mouths of their characters and subjects may be useful to show the extent to which their respective methodologies pervade their works. That is, both Homer and Herodotus present dialogues between individuals, whether divine or human, and the role of questions in such conversations may or may not parallel their authors' own use of questions.

The 112 questions[6] (or question clusters) in the *Iliad* that are pretty surely rhetorical fall into three fairly distinct categories. The largest of these includes a variety of questions asked to focus attention on the speaker's argument.[7] Some are double or even triple, and some have something of taunt or reproach or hint of absurdity, but these are not primary. Most come at the beginning of the particular speech to introduce the argument, but a few come in the middle as a bridge to a new topic or at the end to drive home a point. Examples in Richmond Lattimore's translation are:

Thersites: Son of Atreus, what thing further do you want, or find fault with / now? (2.225)
Nestor: Who knows if, with god helping, you might trouble his spirit / by entreaty? (11.792)
Hector: Have you not all had your glut of being fenced in our outworks? (18.287)
Poseidon: Aineias / which one of the gods is it who urges you to such madness? (20.332)

Parallels in Herodotus include the following:[8]

Gobryas: Dear friends, when will there be a better time to regain the rule? (iii.73.1)
Babylonians: Why do you sit there, men of Persia, and not go away? (iii.151.2)
Ionians: What god have we offended that we suffer in this way? (vi.12.3)
Xerxes: How is it possible for a human being to know anything for sure? (vii.50.2)

A subset of this category is more significant both rhetorically and as demonstrating differences and similarities between Homeric and Herodotean practice. This includes the two-question combinations in which the speaker, having asked one question, proceeds to suggest an answer in a second question. Two examples of the two-question combinations from Homer will serve as illustrations of both form and content:[9]

Achilles: Why have you come now,
         o child of Zeus of the aegis, once more? Is it that you may see
         the outrageousness of the son of Atreus Agamemnon? (1.202)
(Thus the second question provides an answer for the first and itself introduces the speaker's own view of that outrageousness.)

Hera: Sleep, why do you ponder this in your heart, and hesitate?
         Or do you think that Zeus of the wide brows, aiding the Trojans,
         will be angry as he was angry for his son, Herakles? (14.264)
(Hera uses her second question to suggest an answer which will strengthen
her case by lessening Sleep's fear of disobeying Zeus.)

The Herodotean two-question combinations differ from the Homeric
in interesting ways. Although the second questions of both suggest
answers to the first, those of Homer pretend to answer for the person
addressed, attributing motives in a very personal way, speaking as it
were *ad hominem*, while Herodotus' second questions are both less
pointedly personal and tend to develop and define the argument
introduced by the first question. For example:

Darius: Whence came our freedom and who gave it? Was it the populace, an
        oligarchy, or a monarch? (iii.82.5)

Here the answer is obvious; everyone knows that it was Cyrus who
freed the Persians. So Darius can go on to recommend that the way
in which they gained their freedom was the best way to maintain it,
that is, by a monarch. But when Achilles suggests Athena's motive for
coming and when Hera guesses the reason for Sleep's hesitation, the
questioners are not concerned with any answer but only with their
own views. So although the Homeric second question justifies and
motivates what follows, just as Darius' second question does here,
the Homeric question serves only as staging for a display of personal
feelings while the Herodotean question initiates a process of logical
reasoning which makes the rhetorical question less a weapon of personal confrontation than a means of argument and proof.

    Three other examples of two-question combinations in Herodotus'
Histories show the same tendency to logical argument:

Scythian messengers to neighboring chiefs: Will you not do this? If we are
    hard pressed we shall either leave the country or stay and surrender. For
    why are we to suffer if you do not wish to help? (The second question makes

clear the Scythian refusal to bear alone the Persian invasion and introduces the results of non-cooperation for their neighbors.) (iv.118.2)

Mardonius: In fear of what? What kind of assemblage of force? what kind of power of wealth? (The second questions respond to the first and launch an account of the evidence for Greek weakness, since it is not in numbers or in wealth that they are strong.) (vii.9al)

Artemisia: What necessity is there for you to run a risk in sea battles? Do you not already have Athens, for which you came, and the rest of Greece? (The second question makes explicit the answer immanent in the first and introduces evidence of Xerxes' success.) (viii.68a2)

The second category of rhetorical questions in the *Iliad* is made up of accusations involving taunts or reproaches.[10] Most of these are effective in giving impetus to the narrative by inciting the person(s) addressed either to action or to contradiction and justification. On the side of action, for example, Athena impels Odysseus to stem the tide of retreat by asking if the Achaians will flee with their ships and leave Helen as a boast to Priam (2.174), and Odysseus shames Agamemnon into abandoning thought of retreat by asking if he wants to abandon Troy (14.88). Contradiction and justification, on the other hand, are evoked when Agamemnon asks Diomedes why he skulks on the outskirts of battle (4.371), and when Aeneas asks Pandarus where now are his bow and arrows (5.171). In the latter case the reaction is simple, since Pandarus explains and deplores the ineffectiveness of his bow against a divinely protected Diomedes; more complex is the reaction to Agamemnon's taunt, with Sthenelus denying its validity but Diomedes calmly accepting. Whether the questioning of one's hearers' courage or skill results in action or verbal confrontation, the narrative is given impetus or change of direction, and characterization is enhanced. Even when the rhetorical questions have no explicit results they may perform a useful function in the narrative. Thus when Odysseus asks, "Did we not all hear what he (Agamemnon) said in council?" (2.194), the question serves, as no declarative reminder could, to presume the other leaders' assent and cooperation. And when Agamemnon asks the Argives, "Have you no shame? Why do you stand amazed like fauns . . . and do not fight? Or are you waiting for the Trojans to come near . . . so you may see if Zeus protects you?" (4.242), no declarative accusation of the troops in general could provide so effective a background, complete with simile, for the individual reproaches *and* reactions that follow.

Herodotus' use of accusatory rhetorical questions is very different from Homer's, as might be expected from the difference of subject matter. Here is no single grand endeavor where reproach and accusation are limited to the apparent coward and slacker but rather a variety of situations in which accusations are as diverse as the circumstances. Closest to the Homeric kind of accusatory questions are those of the Dream which appears to Xerxes and Artabanus:

Dream: Do you change your mind, Persian, and will you not lead an army against Greece when you have already given mobilization orders? (The statement that follows veils a threat; Xerxes ignores the warning and announces that the expedition is off.) (vii.12.2)

Dream: Son of Darius, do you now come before the Persians renouncing the expedition and paying no heed to my words as if having heard them from someone of no account? (This time a very specific threat follows, and Xerxes is moved to consult his uncle.) (vii.14)

Dream: Are you the one who, on the ground that you have a care for him, discouraged Xerxes from marching against Greece? (There follows a reference to the threat already given Xerxes.) (vii.17.2)

This triad of questions builds to a climax the complex motivation for the campaign against Greece. The complexity involves Xerxes' affirmative decision after pro-and-con speeches by Mardonius and Artabanus and his change after reconsideration to a negative decision that is questioned and reversed with escalating threats by the Dream. The most likely reason for this doubling of motivation is that Herodotus is here judging from the end, following the principle which he has Solon enunciate as a kind of keynote at the beginning of the *Histories* and which is exemplified in his treatment of men and events throughout the work.[11] What ends well or succeeds is what is and so must have been fated and therefore right; what ends badly or fails is what is not and so was neither fated nor right. Thus the Persian expedition against Greece was wrong because it was defeated, but Xerxes must have been right because he survived with no loss of power. Consequently Xerxes as leader of the Persians must at the same time be guilty of wrong and not guilty, and the supernatural questioning with its epic overtones provides the spur to action despite a right decision. Also Homeric is another supernatural accusatory question:

Spirit: Fools, how long will you back water? (The challenge was accepted, and the Greeks began the battle of Salamis.) (viii.84.2)

Other accusatory questions are quite various, having little in common except criticism of speech or action. Two that object to unacceptable demands fail to dissuade and are effective only in characterizing the person making the demand; they are also reminiscent of the epic "What word has crossed the barrier of your teeth?"

Gyges: Lord, what unwholesome word do you speak, bidding me to look at my mistress naked? (i.8.3)

Masistes: What wicked word do you say to me, bidding me divorce my wife, who gave me sons and daughters, one of whom you married to your son, and who besides is very much to my mind—you bid me divorce her and marry your daughter? (ix.111.3)[12]

Two other questions express surprise and shock at words or plans for action and thus perform the truly historical function of clarifying opposing positions by means of presumably fictitious speeches.[13]

Histiaeus (in response to Darius' suggestion that he is responsible for the Ionian Revolt): Lord, what sort of charge have you made, that I plotted something from which you would suffer grievous hurt? What would I be seeking if I did this, and what do I lack? (The second question responds to the first by limiting possible reasons for plotting to dissatisfaction and so introduces an account of Histiaeus' reasons for satisfaction and how he will show his loyalty to Darius. Darius is thus sidetracked into allowing the very treachery he had asked about.) (v.106.2)

Theasides: What are you planning to do, men of Aegina? Carry off the Spartan king now that he is handed over by his fellow-citizens? (The second question by its very phrasing suggests the danger of taking sides in another state's internal affairs. The following statement spells this out: "If now they have condemned him in anger, be on your guard lest at a later time they bring destructive evil on your land." The Aeginetans were moved and employed other tactics to secure the return of their hostages.) (vi.85.2)

Accusatory questions may also lead to threats which in the two following cases are met with a defiance that is important in the understanding of the causes of the East-West conflict.

Persian embassy attacking the men of Croton for refusing to hand over Democedes, a Greek doctor who had made good his escape from Darius: And how will the king like being insulted in this way? How will this be well done by you if you bring harm on yourselves? And against what city shall we campaign before yours and which one will we try to enslave earlier? (The men of Croton are unmoved and thus provide an early example, purposely emphasized by Herodotus as a prefiguring device, of Greek defiance of Persian demands.) (iii.137.3)

Aristagoras, a leader of the Ionian Revolt, in reaction to his Persian col-
league's fury at interference in his command: What business of yours is this
matter? Did not Artaphernes send you to obey me and sail wherever I
ordered? Why are you overbusy? (The veiled threat did not cow the Persian
who proceeded to betray Aristagoras' plans and insure the failure of the
expedition, thus forcing Aristagoras to initiate the Ionian Revolt, at least as
Herodotus presents it.) (v.33.4)

We have come far from the Homeric use of accusatory questions, but
these in the *Histories,* as in the *Iliad,* serve quite literally to question
what is or appears to be wrong and to initiate the business of setting
it right, thus operating as a kinetic factor in the narrative and giving
the impression of causation in the process.

The third category of rhetorical questions employed by Homer,
rather scantily, and by Herodotus, more frequently, includes those
that point up the absurdity of the position taken by the person
addressed. In the *Iliad* Achilles asks Agamemnon (1.123) how the
Achaians will give him a substitute prize, thereby emphasizing the
absurdity of his demand; and Agamemnon asks Achilles (1.133) if
he expects, while he has his own prize, Agamemnon to give up his
and alone be deprived. Each ridicules by means of a question the
preposterous nature of the other's position. Later, when the battle
becomes desperate, Aias attempts to rally the Greeks by questioning
anything on which they might be tempted to rely (15.735):

Do we think there are others who stand behind to help us?
Have we some stronger wall that can rescue men from perdition?

Such questions, although they expect no answer, have more bite than
a simple declarative statement of absurdity.

We have already seen that Herodotus himself used questions that
point up the absurdity of views with which he disagrees. Are the
circumstances similar when he puts such questions in the mouths of
his speakers? Yes, since all of the six speakers who use them do so,
like Achilles, Agamemnon, and Aias, in order to undermine another's conviction or to deflate his expectations.

Atys, on learning that his father is keeping him from the boarhunt because
of a dream that Atys would die wounded by an iron weapon: What kind of
hands does a boar have? Of what sort is the iron weapon you fear? (i.39.2)

Sandanis, warning Croesus against attempting the conquest of the Persians:
If you conquer, what will you get from people who have nothing? (i.71.3)
(It is worth noting here that when Sandanis presents the alternative, which

is an accurate prediction of what is to happen because Croesus does not accept his warning, he speaks declaratively: "And if you are conquered, see how many good things you will lose; for once having sampled them they will not let them go or be turned back." The question is appropriate to deflate expectations, but the warning against what Croesus has not even considered must be stated directly to prefigure the outcome.)

Cambyses, after wounding the Apis with his dagger: Are your gods of such a nature, made of flesh and blood and susceptible to wounds? (iii.29.2) (The absurdity of gods who are mortal and powerless is not made explicit, except in the taunt he goes on to make: "This kind of god is just right for Egyptians.")

Charileos, pointing up the absurdity of his brother Maeandrius' policy: Did you think it right, o worst of men, to cast me in the dungeon, your own brother and innocent of any crime meriting imprisonment, but when you see the Persians trying to evict you and make you homeless, you do not dare to take vengeance even though they are so easy to defeat? (iii.145.2–3) (If we were following Aristotle's classification of rhetorical questions, this would perhaps fall between his category 1, *reductio ad absurdum*, and category 3, showing up self-contradiction, but those distinctions belong to the law courts and assume jurors before whom one's opponent can be discredited. Here in this purely personal confrontation a combination is permissible.)

Darius, after asking the direct and answerable question as to how Zopyrus' self-mutilation would help in the capture of Babylon, then asks: How without taking leave of your senses could you so destroy yourself? (iii.155.3) (The implication is that self-preservation is the very essence of sanity, so that the absurdity is to think that there might be a sane and logical reason for mutilating oneself.)

Xerxes invokes the argument of improbability when he introduces his question with an exhortation to himself: For come let me look at the matter in accordance with all probability; how could a thousand or even ten or fifty thousand men who were all free and not ruled by a single master withstand so great an army as this? (vii.103.3) (The absurdity is clear from Xerxes' point of view and in all physical probability; it is this that makes it both so unanswerable, hence rhetorical, and such an effective comment on the subsequent Greek victory.)

These six questions and situations are in every way comparable to the Homeric challenges on the ground of absurdity. Both Homer and Herodotus use such questions in situations where the speaker attempts to correct misapprehensions and to show up wrong-thinking for what it is. The response to these questions is various and gives some indication of their function in the development of the narrative.

Where there is no response, as in the case of the Egyptians taunted by Cambyses, the chief function seems to be that of characterizing the speaker, who is certainly shown in the event to be unreasonable. Where the hearers are converted, as in the cases of Croesus and the iron weapon and Maeandrius persuaded by Charileos, the questions serve to motivate what because of its disastrous outcome needs extraordinary preparation. Where the hearers reject the imputation of absurdity or unreasonableness, the function of the question depends on whether the charge of absurdity is true or false. If it is true, the hearer who rejects it is understood thereby to incur the penalty of perversity; this would apply to both Agamemnon and Achilles in the *Iliad* and to Croesus in the *Histories* when he rejects Sandanis' advice. If the charge of absurdity is false, the hearers who reject it are vindicated by the event, as in the cases of the sanely self-mutilated Zopyrus and of Demaratus' prediction of Greek fighting spirit. Thus in addition to the rhetorical effectiveness of these questions pointing up absurdity and unreasonableness, there are narrative functions as well, with questions serving as wayside signposts that not only indicate the outcome but also seem to justify it.

One group of Herodotean dialogue-questions is un-Homeric in the extreme. Although these have something of the *reductio ad absurdum* in their make-up, their chief function is as anecdotal punchline. In three cases this is built up to in a syllogistic fashion; the fourth, in the form of a prayer to Zeus, with whom back-chat is not possible, stands alone.

(The scene: Croesus is building ships to campaign against the islands. Bias: The islanders are buying horses to march against Sardis. Croesus: God grant that they come with cavalry against the Lydians. Bias: You pray to catch the islanders on horseback . . .) What else do you think the islanders pray for . . . than to catch the Lydians on the sea . . . ? (i.27.4)

(The scene: the Hellespont where Xerxes' counselors urge him to capture Greek grain ships passing through. Xerxes: Where are the ships going? Counselors: They go to your enemy.) Xerxes: Are not we too going there, carrying grain among other things? What harm then do they do transporting food for us? (vii.147.3)

(The scene: Arcadian deserters arrive in the Persian camp. A Persian: What are the Greeks doing? Deserters: They are holding the Olympic games. Persian: For what prizes do they contend? Deserters: A crown of olive.) Tritantaechmes: Against what sort of men have you brought us to fight,

Mardonius, who strive not for the sake of wealth but for virtue's sake? (viii.26.3)

(The scene: the Hellespont after Xerxes' army has crossed into Europe.) A local man: O Zeus, why do you take on human shape and the name of Xerxes instead of Zeus in order to overthrow Greece, leading all mankind? For even without these you could do it. (vii.56.2)

Unlike other questions that take their place as part of a speech's argument either motivating action or justifying outcome, these punchline questions, complete with build-up, are outside the causal nexus of events and could be omitted without affecting the orderly and consecutive flow of the narrative. In this respect these four anecdotes are the antitheses of the clever-answer motivating drama[14] which at its most basic follows this form: (1) Persian king acts in conformity with his position or despotically; (2) person affected reacts unexpectedly; (3) king makes inquiry; (4) answer produces reversal or cancellation of original action. The purest example is: (1) Cambyses tests Psammenitus by forcing him to see his daughter humiliated and his son sent off to execution; (2) Psammenitus shows no emotion at these sights but weeps when he sees an old comrade reduced to beggary; (3) Cambyses asks why he behaves so; (4) Psammenitus' answer that his own suffering was too great for tears motivates Cambyses to countermand his previous orders and welcome Psammenitus to his court (iii.14.9–10).

Almost identical except in its result is the anecdote (iii.32.2) in which (1) Cambyses stages a combat between a lion cub and a puppy; (2) when the cub is winning and the puppy's brother breaks its chain and comes to help, Cambyses' sister-wife weeps; (3) Cambyses asks why; (4) her answer—that it was because he no longer had a brother to come to his aid—should cause him to countermand his order for his brother's murder, but because this is one of several anecdotes proving his madness it motivates instead his murder of the sister-wife. This is a good example of the way in which a normal pattern used inappropriately can point up abnormality.

Other examples of the pattern repeat steps 3 and 4, since the first clever answer is so obscure as to require a second question: (1) Darius, suspecting conspiracy, imprisons Intaphernes and all his male relatives; (2) Intaphernes' wife weeps continuously outside the palace; (3) Darius in pity asks her to choose one relative to be saved; (4) she chooses her brother; (3a) Darius asks why; (4a) her answer—that she can get other husbands and sons but not another brother since her parents are dead—causes Darius to give her both brother and son (iii.119.3–6).[15]

Returning now to the more specifically rhetorical question, it appears that, generally speaking, for both Homer and Herodotus a speaker's point is sharpened if it pins down the person addressed, and a question does this much more effectively than a declarative statement. Whether the question demonstrates absurdity, makes an accusation of wrong-headedness, or simply provides an opening for the questioner's own answer, it captures the attention of the person addressed and, from the audience's point of view, involves him in confrontation and puts him on the spot. By and large, Homer's use is both more limited in variety of situations and less logical in argument. The great development of the rhetorical question in Herodotus' *Histories* undoubtedly came along not only with the enlargement of the human scene to include unheroic everyday confrontations and the forms of discourse practiced in them but also with Herodotus' own fairly rigorous pursuit of answers to his inquiries. For both the questions that Herodotus himself asks and those that he puts into the mouths of others are powerful tools in the search for truth or probability and in the achievement of right action, since they penetrate appearances, open matters to debate, and subject actions to scrutiny. Some may conclude a discussion, punchline fashion, and after careful build-up bring sudden enlightenment. Others may initiate discussion, debate fashion, and launch the argumentation against misapprehension. In any case the use of the question is a reflection, in miniature, of the work of the historian as Herodotus saw it—to inquire, to learn, and to examine. At the same time, questions are but one of the many means by which speeches in the *Histories* combine with Herodotus' narrative style to present actions and events with so much verisimilitude that the reader must be on his guard if he at all believes that truth is stranger than fiction.

Chapter 4

Look to the End

We have seen something of the way in which Herodotus' record of events was affected by his narrative style and by his use of direct and indirect discourse. Then a survey of rhetorical questions in Herodotus' narrative and dialogue compared with those in the *Iliad* helped to show a development of thought and style that further influenced the presentation of the material of Herodotus' inquiry. Now an examination of how two other rhetorical devices function in the *Histories* will define more closely Herodotus' role as intermediary between past and future, between the largely oral and the indubitably literate. In Herodotus' presentation of alternative courses of action in both speech and narrative we see foreshadowed the Thucydidean debates that clarify issues and rationalize choices. And in Herodotus' use of maxims, proverbs, or commonplaces we see the continued operation and influence of traditional folk wisdom. By surveying the nature and effects of these rather different ways of realizing and coping with situations we can come to a fuller appreciation of the direction that Herodotus has given to the *Histories*.

The simplest form in which a choice can be presented is the alternative question. In the *Histories* alternative questions are almost invariably phrased in such a way that the alternative that will be chosen comes first and thus serves to introduce or foreshadow the result. What then is the function of the second alternative? It seems both to provide a context of potentiality and to serve as a foil emphasizing by contrast the one chosen. In the most straightforward examples the second alternative appears only in the question and is ignored in the answer, so that the order is *aba*:[1]

Croesus: Should I say what I think or be silent? (i.88.2) (Cyrus urges him to say what he wishes.)

Demaratus: Shall I tell the truth or what you want to hear? (vii.101.3) (Xerxes urges him to tell the truth.)

Slightly more complicated is the *abba* order that leads from the first alternative through presentation and disposal of the second back to the first as the one that will point the way to the next narrative item:

Periander to his son: Which is better, your present squalor or the prospect of riches and power? . . . Go home, having learned how much better it is to be envied than pitied. (iii.52.3) (The squalor-riches-envy-pity sequence gives an *abba* order, leading to the son's implicit choice of squalor when he charges his father with having disobeyed his own edict by speaking to him.)

Other examples of both *aba* and *abba* alternative questions are extended by a third interchanging pair, *ababba* or *abbaba*. Whatever the alternation, however, the matter to be motivated or explained is carried by *a*, bruited in the beginning and both confirmed and effective at the end, while *b* provides contrast and context.

(Cyrus asks whether they preferred the previous day's toil or the present feast. They answer that yesterday was all bad and today all good.) Cyrus: The goods are all yours if you wish to obey me; if you do not, you will have unlimited toil like yesterday's. (i.126.3) (The *ababba* order is toil-feast-bad-good-goods-toil, with toil used to motivate revolt at the same time as it is given impetus by contrast with goods.)

Xerxes: What two things are most hostile to me? Is my infantry inadequate? Or is my fleet? Or both? Artabanus: Neither army nor fleet is inferior; it is the land and the sea that I fear; the sea because of such-and-such, the land because of so-and-so. (vii.48) (Here a fourth pair is added in order to make the transition from army to land and fleet to sea: *abab, abba* or army-fleet-army-fleet-land-sea-sea-land.)

These five alternative questions (and six others that are comparable)[2] all lead with the alternative that will be effective either as motivation or explanation and show the way in which the narrative builds up to actions or situations gradually, providing the raw materials, as it were, out of which they developed. Four other questions presenting alternatives lead to answers that accept neither, thus giving what amounts to three possibilities. One example (v.82.2) will suffice:[3]

The Epidaurians ask whether they should make the statues of bronze or of stone. The oracle says neither, but of olive wood.

Here the alternatives serve not as lead-in and foil to what follows but rather to evoke rejection and thus open the way for what might be thought a least likely possibility. The third and realized possibility is not an immediately obvious one and can be most convincingly introduced by a rejection of two more likely possibilities, like stone or bronze for statues.

More complex than alternative questions are the choices between alternative courses of action that are presented in speeches. These are unlike the consideration of alternatives both reported and quoted in the _Iliad_ where it is the actor himself who debates whether to retreat or to stand fast (11.404; 17.91; 21.553; 22.99), whether to seek help or go it alone (13.455; 14.20), or whether to pursue some particular object or to kill more of the enemy (5.671; 10.503). Because the Homeric soliloquy is a useful device for presenting not only an isolated hero's options but also his state of mind, it may have influenced Herodotus in his use of alternatives; but the shift from internal debate to dramatic dialogue surely owes much to other sources as well. It is in speeches of command, appeal, advice, or proposal that alternatives are presented in the _Histories_, and that Herodotus found them effective both as a means of persuasion and as a vehicle of interpretation is attested by their frequency. That is, any action taken as a result of a speech including such a choice is thereby set in a context of the options. The presentation of alternatives gives focus to the command, appeal, advice, or proposal and at the same time dramatizes the decision. In addition, by putting such a speech in the mouth of a speaker, Herodotus provides in an informal fashion the kind of overview of the issues and potentialities of the situation that Thucydides was later to formalize and elaborate in opposing speeches on the issues. Thus a speech that outlines the alternatives not only presents its hearer with a choice but also gives the reader insight into the possibilities of a situation. This is particularly true when the speaker adds to his outline of alternatives some account of the results that are to be expected if one or the other is chosen. The rationale is clearly spelled out in the proemion of Artabanus' speech opposing Mardonius (vii.10a1):

> O king, if opposing views are not expressed, it is not possible for the one choosing to take the better course, but he must follow the one that is suggested. When both are expressed, it is possible to recognize the better view, just as we only recognize pure gold when we rub it against other gold.[4]

Artabanus is here justifying the expression of an opposing point of view by a second speaker, but the principle holds equally for alternatives presented by a single speaker. This latter kind of presentation is far more frequent in the *Histories*, partly at least because the kind of opposition that Artabanus exemplifies is virtually limited to the special situation in which a warning speech opposing a speech of persuasion is ignored. It is almost invariably true that actions or undertakings that will be successful are preceded only by speeches of persuasion or challenge, and no opposite view is expressed. Indeed, the introduction of a speaker presenting arguments against an undertaking is one of Herodotus' methods of explaining and justifying its failure, since refusal to heed a warning demonstrates the kind of blindness (*ate*) that leads to ruin. With this specialized use of the *agon* between *peitho*[5] and a tragic warner, the presentation of two sides to a question or of mutually exclusive actions almost had to be handled differently; hence the single speech with its offer of alternatives.

The simplest speeches presenting alternatives merely state the two possible or desirable courses of action without urging one or the other and without elaborating on the results that either course will involve or implying anything about the morality or expediency of either. Sample speeches illustrate ways of presenting alternatives that provide both impetus for the decision and the context in which it must be made:

Queen: Either kill Candaules and possess both me and the kingdom, or you yourself must die so that you do not in the future see what you should not . . . Either he who planned this thing or you who did it must die. (i.11)

Tomyris: Either cross over here while we withdraw, or if you wish to receive us, you withdraw. (i.206)

Again in these and in other similar examples[6] the alternative that will be chosen is given first. In only one case is the order reversed, perhaps because the proposal is so preposterous that it turns even an established formula inside out. This is when the Ionian fleet is sent to help the Cypriotes during the Ionian Revolt:

Cypriote tyrants: We give you a choice between fighting on land against the Persians or at sea with the Phoenicians. (*ab*)
Ionians: Our duty is to guard the sea rather than to fight on land. (*ba*) (v.109)

That the pattern of alternatives may have been used here almost automatically even though there was no real choice is suggested by the next example, which follows after only a few lines of narrative and similarly opens up to choice an arrangement that would ordinarily be taken for granted:

> Onesilus (expecting to do battle with the opposing commander, Artybius, whose horse was trained to savage footsoldiers, to his attendant): Say which you want to attack, Artybius' horse or the man himself. (*ab*)
> Attendant: Artybius is an opponent suitable for you; I will take on the horse. (*ba*)
> (v.111)

Some ten speeches present alternatives in order to urge one course of action by indicating both its potentially good results and the bad results of the other.[7] If only motivation had been Herodotus' aim, persuasion toward the one course would have sufficed; nor are the two alternatives presented in order to give an illusion of choice, since the decision is so strongly influenced. The real and effective purpose of the alternative is to give the reader, not the person addressed, the potentialities of the situation, to clarify the resulting decision and prefigure the results.

> Cambyses: Do not overlook the passing of Persian power to the Medes; if you regain it, may all goods come to you; if you do not, I call down on you all curses. (iii.65.6–7)

The following narrative is given direction by the force of the *abba* pattern, so that after those Persians who made no push to regain power are dealt with, there is the account of the Seven Conspirators who did as Cambyses wished. The first alternative predicts the first result, and the *abba* order shows that the speech's function is less to motivate the Persian coup than to provide narrative transition from Cambyses' loss of power to the conspirators' plot to regain it.

> Persian envoys (to the deposed Ionian tyrants): Seduce your fellow citizens from the rebel cause and proclaim that they will thus fare better, but that if they do not give up the revolt, they will suffer terribly. (vi.9.3–4)

This speech, with abandoning the revolt as *a* and persisting in it as *b*, leads us to expect the narrative to continue with the Ionians abandoning the revolt (*a*). But here the *abba* pattern operates more broadly: it introduces the Ionians refusal to listen to the tyrants and their persistence in the revolt. And that persistence is exemplified in the story of the Phocaean general's insistence on their training for battle for long hours under the hot sun. But then, when all of them rebelled against this toil, some were ready to listen to their deposed tyrants and abandon the revolt. Thus the first alternative serves as a long-distance prediction of Samian defection and the failure of the revolt, while the second alternative introduces a near-distance example of Ionian persistence that, by a kind of backfire, is the apparent cause of abandoning the revolt. This is narrative prestidigitation by which the illusion of historical causation is achieved through what is chiefly a convenient and patterned form of transition.

Another speech that plays an important part in narrative transition is the one that apparently determines Athenian participation in the battle of Marathon:

Miltiades: It is in your power either to enslave Athens or make her free (*ab*). Now if the Athenians yield to the Persians they will be handed over to Hippias, but if the city survives it will be the first in Greece (*ab*). If we do not fight, there will be pressure to medize; if we do fight now, we can survive (*ab*). If you side with me, our fatherland will be free and first in Greece; if you choose the other side, it will be the opposite (*ba*). (vi.109.3–6)

The reversal of the usual order, in which the alternative to be chosen is given first, must result from the transitional function of the speech, which serves as a pivot and effects a turnabout from the Athenian reluctance to their readiness to face the Persians. Thus again what is a convenient transition—this time from the generals' majority opinion against fighting to the decision to meet the Persians—appears to be the cause of that decision.

Comparison with the presentation of alternatives to the Spartan general by Themistocles before Salamis shows that when the purpose of the speech is confirmation of the current position rather than shift or turnabout, the first alternative given is the one to be chosen and so to lead the way or make the transition to the outcome.

Themistocles: It is in your power to save Greece if you do battle here and do not retreat to the Isthmus (*ab*). The dangers of fighting at the Isthmus must be considered in contrast to the advantages of fighting here (*ba*). Staying here you will be right; if not, you will destroy Greece (*ab*). If you do not stay, we Athenians shall depart to seek our fortune elsewhere (*b*). (viii.60–62) (The Spartan general's decision to stay and fight completes the second *abba*. That his decision follows directly on Themistocles' threat and so was chiefly motivated by it is immediately confirmed by Herodotus' own comment that it was this fear that influenced him. Thus the speech is seen quite clearly to represent what Herodotus thought was necessary [*ta deonta*].)

Five other speeches presenting alternatives do so apparently to give fair warning of disaster if one of the two is chosen.[8] The disaster is thus prefigured for the reader even as heedlessness of the warning brings it on. The only reason for the inclusion of the harmless alternative seems to be the pull of the pattern with its effect of contrast. For example:

Sandanis: If you win, what will you gain from those who have nothing? But if you are defeated, see how many good things you will lose. (i.71.2–4)[9]

Thus the Herodotean use of alternatives fulfills both dramatic and narrative functions. It gives narrative cohesion in one of two ways. Where the movement is circular and the former alternative is finally adopted, the identity of the two ends serves to bracket even a fairly extensive examination of the second choice and prevent the narrative from seeming to go off on a tangent. Where the movement is linear, starting with one alternative and ending with the other, the use of choice between the two makes possible a kind of narrative about-face without loss of continuity. At the same time, by dramatizing the decision, the dialogue involves the reader and defines the parameters of the particular situation. In this regard particularly, Herodotus seems to form a bridge between the heroic soliloquy of the *Iliad* and the issue-debates in Thucydides.

Folk wisdom, or maxims, constitutes a second device that shows up Herodotus as a middleman between tradition and science. If, as Francis Bacon thought, "the genius, wit and spirit of a nation are discovered in its proverbs," how fortunate we are in having a Greek historian who makes much use of the folk wisdom of his people and so gives us the opportunity to make this discovery. And because Herodotus introduces proverb-like sayings in both narrative and speeches, we can not only glimpse the use as well as the nature of these commonplaces but also discern the extent to which a historian nurtured in this way views the course of events in their light.[10] That is, the proverbs that his speakers use and the way in which they use them to persuade, to warn, and to justify may, in some degree at least, reflect the genius, wit, and spirit of the Greek nation. And his own use of such proverbs in the narrative may demonstrate the extent to which his interpretation of events and view of causation were shaped by this inherited folk widsom.

A first difficulty will be in defining what a proverb is and in determining which among many general statements in the *Histories* may be classified as proverbs. *Paroimia* is used by both Aeschylus (*Ag.* 264) and Sophocles (*Ajax* 664) to designate what we would call a proverb. And *gnome* seems to be used already in the fifth century B.C. in the general sense of our "maxim" or the Latin *sententia*. But since Herodotus uses neither *gnome* in this sense nor *paroimia*, we have no sample of what he might have so defined. Identifying what Herodotus and his readers regarded as maxims or proverbs therefore involves finding other criteria. In two cases, fortunately, he gives a sufficiently explicit introduction to make the identification as maxims clear:

> Long ago men discovered what things were good, and we ought to learn from them; one of these is: look to your own. (i.8.4)
> Therefore take to heart also how well said is the old saying: the end is not seen in the beginning. (vii.51.3)

If we use the clues provided both by these two introductions and by the format of the two sayings thereby validated as maxims, we can spread a larger net to catch other possible proverbial sayings. Then, using both the format of these and their introductions to draw in still others, and so on, we may make a fair collection. That is, on the basis of these two we shall include as maxims all those general statements that are introduced by a command to take to heart or by a verb of learning and, by extension, by verbs knowing, perceiving, and understanding. And as far as the format of the maxims themselves is concerned, we may identify others that similarly employ imperative verbs or infinitives either functioning as imperatives or used with an article as a substantive. Using these criteria we collect some twenty-one sayings, of which the following are a sample:[11]

Injustice is the enemy of justice. (i.96.2)
Desire of many things is evil. (vii.18.2)
A man's spirit dwells in his ears. (vii.39.1)
All human life is brief. (vii.46.2)
Good masters have bad servants and bad masters good. (viii.68g)
There is neither faith nor truth in foreigners. (viii.142.5)
The Spartans think one thing and say another. (ix.54.1)

The twenty-one in turn provide new criteria—for example, general statements based on a neuter adjective with or without the verb "to be" and an infinitive, and general statements based on verbs with the "be accustomed" meaning or with a construction comparable to the imperative, like an impersonal verb of necessity. These bring in another twenty-six, of which the following are samples:[12]

No man is ever self-sufficient. (i.32.8)
Treaties seldom remain intact without powerful sanctions. (i.74.4)
It is better, daring all, to suffer half the time than, fearing, have nothing. (vii.50.1)
Great affairs are wont to involve great risks. (vii.50.3)
Reproaches provoke a man's anger. (vii.160.1)
It is not easy to give the best advice. (viii.102.1)
It is better to end one's life accomplishing something by defending it than giving in to perish miserably. (ix.17.4)
Soft lands are wont to produce soft men. (ix. 122.3)

These add two new criteria that bring in thirteen more sayings,[13] making a total of sixty plus our original two. Then to these sixty-two it is tempting to add twelve more examples, ten because they sound like maxims[14] and two because they incorporate sentiments similar to sayings already collected.[15] In their Herodotean, or applied, form, many of these seventy-four are not pure general statements but have suffered alternations of mood or case or additions of particles or particularizing nouns in order to serve the specific purpose of their quotation. So, for example, a sententious modern historian might write, "Pride went before Napoleon's fall." But even after all of this particularizing material is removed, the general statements that are left may still not qualify as maxims. It is time, therefore, to seek out a definition by which the seventy-four general statements we have gathered from the *Histories* may be judged.

Reinhold Strömberg's description is useful here: "The most conspicuous features of the genuine *paroimia* are: it is current among the people: *demotikon kai koinon* (Demetrius *de elocut.* 232); it usually has concise brevity, *syntomia* (Aristotle, fr. 13 Rose) and *glykytes* (Aristides *Rhet.* p. 499,22); it is by nature a *charien pragma* (Demetrius *1.c.* 156), sometimes *didaktikon*, usually *pithanon*, sometimes enigmatic, cryptic and difficult to decipher."[16] Another paremiologist, B. J. Whiting, distinguishes as follows between popular proverbs and learned proverbs or sentences (*sententiae*): "A proverb is an expression which owes its birth to the people and testifies to its origin in form and phrase whereas a sentence is a piece of wisdom which has not crystallized into specific current form and which anyone feels free to rephrase to suit himself."[17] And though it is convenient to use the term "maxim" for both popular proverbs and sentences, we would do well to attempt a division between them. This may be most easily accomplished by first classifying them according to subject matter so that we may distinguish those "pieces of wisdom that have not been crystallized" from those that have come into the literature already in a steady state.

In the process of dealing with categories of subject matter it will be convenient to examine the ways in which maxims are used, both rhetorically and historically. And since the concept of divine jealousy is so closely tied to Herodotus' philosophy of history in the minds of many, the maxims which assert this as a force to be reckoned with will make a good beginning. Divine jealousy appears in four speeches: both Solon (i.32.1) and Amasis (iii.40.2) refer to themselves as "knowing that divinity is jealous," using the same words; and Artabanus (vii.46.4) says that god is jealous of sharing his blessedness. This last seems to be embroidery on the "divinity is jealous" of the first two, which because of its verbatim repetition and brevity should be a popular proverb. But when Artabanus (vii.103) describes the effects of divine jealousy, indicating the way in which god destroys the largest animals, the tallest buildings and trees, and allows no competition, this might best be called a *sententia*, or a piece of wisdom that could be specifically phrased, as here, to show how Xerxes' vast host was of the size that invited destruction. What is most notable about this divine jealousy is the use to which Herodotus puts it: in addition to the four places just noted, it occurs again in only one other speech when Themistocles argues (viii.109.3) that Xerxes' defeat resulted from divine jealousy of his attempt to rule both Asia and Europe; nowhere in his narrative does Herodotus himself attribute to divine jealousy the defeat or fall of any great leader who might have been thought to be exceeding human limits.[18]

The divine-jealousy maxim is used in the way maxims tend to be used: as a short-cut exposition of a speaker's point of view and to prop up an argument by appealing, as it were, to the authority of popular belief. That, at any rate, is the implication of the earliest definition of *paroimiai*, attributed to Aristotle by Synesius (*Calv. Encom.* 22): "remnants of the ancient philosophy which survived because of their brevity and wit." Herodotus has both Solon and Amasis explain their warnings against taking good fortune for granted as based on their knowledge of divine jealousy, but that does not mean that the historian sees the subsequent fall of both Croesus and Polycrates as caused by divine jealousy. As a matter of fact, he most explicitly attributes their defeats to their own very human error. Thus although this particular maxim has a very definite rhetorical value, like Pindar's "Let him not seek to become a god" (*Ol.* 5.24), it has no merit for Herodotus as an expression of historical causation. Similarly, the divine jealousy about which Artabanus warns and to which Themistocles attributes Xerxes' fall has the rhetorical function of validating Greek victory without being historically effective.

Far different from the maxims warning against divine jealousy used by Herodotean speakers are the proverbs or general statements in which Homer's heroes refer to the gods' role in their affairs. The emphasis there is also, to be sure, on the gods' power and their superiority to men, but they are not thought of as expecting or resenting rivalry from men, except when on occasion one divinity urges a hero to oppose another divinity. A typical general statement is spoken by both Automedon (17.514) and Hector (20.435) in the *Iliad* and by Athena (1.267) and Telemachus (16.129) in the *Odyssey:* "These things lie on the lap of the gods." And Menelaus points out, "The immortal gods hold the threads of victory" (*Il.* 7.102). Both Homer himself (*Il.* 16.688) and Hector (*Il.* 17.176) assert, "Always the mind of Zeus is stronger," showing that what is proverbial for the heroes is proverbial for the poet, unlike the difference demonstrated in the *Histories* between Herodotus and his speakers' use of divine jealousy. It is possible that hints of the divine-jealousy notion can be found in Homer; thus Menelaus will not let Telemachus compare his palace to that of Zeus (*Od.* 4.78–81) and Apollo warns Diomedes, "Do not wish to have thoughts equal to the gods" (*Il.* 5.440–441). But the lack of explicit statement and actual words suggests that the real growth of the folk wisdom out of which the divine-jealousy proverb sprang either belonged to the peasant culture ignored by heroic poetry or came out of the social and economic upheavals of the seventh and sixth centuries B.C. On the other hand, the close similarity of some Homeric and Herodotean maxims suggests that some attitudes were too basically human to be affected by cultural differences and social upheaval. So, for example, Homer's "Victory changes sides" (*Il.*

6.339) is echoed in a variety of Herodotean maxims concerned with the uncertainty or instability of the human condition. Four of these emphasize mutability:

Human happiness never stays long in the same place. (i.5.4) (Herodotus is justifying the inclusion in the *Histories* of both great and small cities.)

Man is all chance. (i.32.4) (Solon summarizes the point he is making to Croesus.)

There is a wheel of human affairs which as it revolves does not allow the same men always to be fortunate. (i.207.2) (Croesus supports his warning against overconfidence.)

How is it possible for a human being to know certainty? (vii.50.2) (Xerxes justifies taking a risk.)

Although the points made in these four expressions are similar, the language is so different and so appropriate to the particular use that there is no question here of a proverb but rather the uncrystallized expression of a *sententia* or *gnome*. Two other maxims deal with the ends of things, and another two touch on other aspects of uncertainty:

It is right to look how every affair comes out at the end. (i.32.9) (Solon supports his warning to Croesus.)

Every end is not apparent at the beginning. (vii.51.3) (Artabanus supports a warning.)

Our affairs are on a razor's edge. (vi.11.2) (Dionysius justifies proposed action. Compare *Iliad* 10.173, "Now the outcome stands on a razor's edge for all.")

Circumstance rules men, not men circumstance. (vii.49.3) (Artabanus supports his warning to Xerxes.)

It may be that Artabanus' expressions about the end as not apparent at the beginning and circumstance ruling men as well as Dionysius' razor's edge are truly proverbial since they have the brevity and wit the definitions require. And obviously the uncertainty of human affairs is a broad enough subject to give rise to a variety of proverbs, but even so common and specific an idea as Solon's "look to the end" is given sufficiently different expression by fifth-century tragedians to suggest that crystallization was still in process:

Think the man happy who ends his life well. (Aeschylus, *Ag.* 928–929)

Looking to the end, count no man happy until he finishes his life without pain. (Sophocles, *OT* 1528–30)

Never say any man is happy until you see how he comes to his final day. (Euripides, *Androm.* 100–101)

As we have seen, these *gnomai* about life's uncertainty are used in the *Histories* in three different ways: to justify proposed action, to support warning, and to summarize or cap an argument. The fact that Herodotus himself uses the fluctuation of human fortunes in much the same way as Dionysius or Xerxes makes it appear that he considers it a fact of history as well as rhetorically useful. The same is largely true of four expressions dealing with the inescapability of fate:

Even a god cannot escape what is fated. (i.91.1) (The oracle explains Apollo's failure to save Croesus.)
It is impossible to save a man from what is coming to him. (iii.43.1) (Herodotus explains that Amasis, having learned this, gave up on Polycrates.)
It is not humanly possible to turn aside what is going to be. (iii.65.3) (Cambyses explains why he failed to save his throne.)
It is not possible to turn aside whatever is fated to come from god. (ix.16.4) (A Persian explains his failure to warn Mardonius.).[19]

As the circumstances differ, so the vocabulary shifts, ringing the changes on *adunaton-amechanon* and *apotrepein-ekkomisai;* and the situation ranges from god's inability to escape fate to human helplessness to avert what comes from the gods. All seem to be *gnomai,* but no one is proverbial. Herodotus' own use again suggests, as does the role he gives oracles in the *Histories,* that the rhetorical convenience of fate's inescapability as an explanation of failure to act effectively may have contributed to his apparent historical belief that what is had to be.

Of fifteen *gnomai* dealing with right action, six concern the value of counsel.[20] Three samples give the range:[21]

Counseling well brings greatest gain. (vii.10d2)
Being wise and being willing to heed good advice are pretty much the same thing. (vii.16a)
The end of a well-thought-out matter tends to be good. (vii.157.3)

All six give various expression to a general idea and so are merely gnomic; all six are in speeches, three by Artabanus and the others by Megabyzus, Themistocles, and the Greek envoys to Gelon, all justifying their offer of advice. It is uncertain whether Herodotus' own view of the value of counsel resulted more from maxim-engendered conviction or from his narrative's need for dramatic confrontations between advisers and advisees.

The following more miscellaneous general statements about right action have a higher proportion of true maxims, dealing as they do with more various circumstances and so not needing variety of expression:[22]

A man should look to his own. (i.8.4) (Gyges justifies his refusal.)
Forethought is a wise thing. (iii.36.1) (Croesus supports a warning.)
Do not cure ill with ill. (iii.53.4) (Periander's daughter justifies her advice.)
Most valuable of all possessions is a wise and loyal friend. (v.24.3) (Darius
explains his invitation to Histiaeus. Homer's version, spoken by Agamemnon to Nestor, is, "Worth a great host is a man whom Zeus loves in
his heart"—*Il.* 9.116–117.)
Nothing is automatic but from trying all things come to men. (vii.9g) (Mardonius urges action.)

Detailed consideration of the other maxims[23] still more miscellaneous in subject matter is unnecessary since it is clear from the
examples already noted that Herodotus' use of them both in narrative
and in speeches is largely justificatory, either of a point being made
by the speaker or of the action to be taken. Thus whether the maxim
is used to support a warning, to explain a point being made, or to urge
a course of action, it applies a generally accepted truth to the particular situation and so puts it in a context that lends conviction. I think
it is worthwhile, however, to point out a few more of the maxims that
are most like proverbs, both to see if they are ever used differently and
to ask why they, unlike the *gnomai*, do not appear in the narrative but
only in speeches.

Men's ears are less trustworthy than their eyes. (i.8.2) (Candaules endeavors
to persuade Gyges, using an almost proverbial form of what Heracleitus
expressed thus: "Eyes are more accurate witnesses than ears"—Diels B.
101a.)
A woman puts off her modesty with her clothes. (i.8.3) (Gyges uses another
proverb to explain and justify his reluctance to obey.)

Croesus employs in expanded form what became a proverbial jingle,
at least at a later time, *pathei mathos*, and what was a widespread
gnome in the sixth and fifth centuries; Croesus' version is, "My sufferings, being bitter, have become lessons" (i.207.1).[24] Aesop uses as
a moral the wording "Often sufferings become lessons for men"
(Hausrath 134, 223). And Aeschylus speaks of "learning through suffering" (*Ag.* 177). Croesus' use of the maxim is to explain and justify
his readiness to advise Cyrus.

Periander's plea to his son includes the statement "It is better to be
envied than pitied" (iii.52.5), which echoes a maxim familiar from
Pindar, "But still envy is better than pity" (*Pyth.* i.85). Darius explains
his request for a volunteer who can employ craft with the following:
"Where there is need of cleverness force is out of place" (iii.127.2).
And the Thessalians justify their refusal to stand alone against the

Persian invasion: "For necessity is never stronger than power-lessness" (vii.172.3).

Other possible maxims are used somewhat differently in that their primary purpose seems to be to deliver a threat, not openly but in the veiled form of a general statement:

> You sewed the sandal, and Aristagoras put it on. (vi.1.2) (Artaphernes thus makes it clear to Histiaeus that he knows that though Aristagoras leads the revolt it was Histiaeus who instigated it.)
> Rub out like a pine tree. (vi.37.2) (Croesus threatens to do this to the Lamp-sacenes if they do not release Miltiades.)
> The spring is taken out of the year. (vii.162.1) (Gelon makes this parallel for the Greek army without the Sicilian contingent. The much debated question whether Herodotus has here borrowed from Pericles seems to me irrelevant. Surely it is obvious that this proverb was in the public domain and could be used, more or less aptly, in any situation involving loss of one's best hope.)
> In the games those who jump the starting-signal are punished. (viii.59) (Adeimantus chides Themistocles for speaking out of turn in Council.)
> Those who are left behind are not crowned. (viii.59) (Themistocles answers.)

That Herodotus himself does not use true proverbs in his narrative is more understandable when we see this use in making threats. And in other cases where proverb-like maxims are used to support warnings or to justify the speaker's position, they often seem designed to put the hearer in the wrong by imputing error, folly, or willful wrong-doing, even though they do not make the charge explicit. Obviously, such a use would have no place in Herodotus' narrative, and with one significant exception true proverbs seem to have little or no historical dimension. That exception, the "look to the end" of our title, is basic to Herodotus' interpretation of events. Not only does he judge under-takings by their outcome, but often he seems to divine purposes from results. This latter practice has been shared by many of Herodotus' successors, beginning with Thucydides, at whose use of *gnomai* we should now look in order to demonstrate more clearly Herodotus' position as middleman between past and future, between tradition and science.

The proverbs that the ancient paremiographers found in Thucy-dides' work are not only far fewer than those we have seen in Herod-otus' *Histories* but qualitatively different as well. Most seem to have become proverbs only after the Thucydidean expression of a complex and paradoxical truth became recognized as such:

Peace is stronger when it comes out of war, but not to turn to war from peace is not equally without risk. (i.124.2) (The Corinthians are urging the Spartans to war.)

It is more shameful for reputable men to make gains by specious fraud than by open force, for the one is with the rightness of fortune-given might, the other with the scheming of unjust intent. (iv.86.6) (Brasidas is justifying Spartan attacks on Thracian cities.)

These, like the following, also serve to characterize the speakers and show them making the "worse appear the better reason." Thus Cleon is given what might well be a true Spartan *gnome:*

Cautious ignorance is more useful than undisciplined cleverness. (iii.37.3)

And in his answer Diodotus represents the Athenian ideal:

For planning well against an opponent is more effective than going to work with mindless force. (iii.48.2)

Thus Thucydides seems to be not so much a user of traditional maxims as an inventor of sophistic *gnomai* which he gives to his speakers to characterize them and their purposes in the very same way in which Herodotus gives his speakers bits of folk wisdom. That some of those bits have not yet been crystallized into proverbs and that Herodotus plays an important part in that crystallization helps to put him squarely in the middle of the paremiographic stream.

Finally, coming back to that proverb that he helped to make even as it gave a shape to his *Histories,* let us look to the end and so back to the beginning, for "look to the end" is as basic to Herodotus' narrative style as it is to his historical interpretation. As the arrow aims and the carrot attracts, so the topic sentence looks ahead to the end of an episode and holds together an account which can enclose a variety of digressive material that looks to that same end. In the same way it is the end of a man or an affair that determines Herodotus' introduction and interpretation. So who is to wonder if what had been uncrystallized general *sententiae* about the importance of the end were converted into an actual proverb during the fifth century in the climate of opinion that nurtured and was nurtured by Herodotus and the tragedians?

Epilogue

In this work, when it shall be found that much is omitted,
let it not be forgotten that much likewise is performed.

Samuel Johnson, Preface to the
English Dictionary, 1755

In the foregoing chapters various approaches to Herodotean narrative and discourse have been briefly explored in an effort to suggest the extent to which the oral style and nature of both Homeric epic, as his poetic model, and oral tradition, as his chief source, are exemplified in the *Histories*. Most obvious is the importance given to direct discourse and the consequent dramatization of personal interaction and confrontation. Furthermore, the speeches and dialogues themselves incorporate oral features, being patterned in form and used formulaically, as has been indicated in Chapter 2. As far as content is concerned, little has been attempted here, but much could be done using Herodotus' speeches to formulate a kind of proto-rhetoric that would reflect the amateur argumentation of oral tradition and poetics. Regular elements of this proto-rhetoric, used both to persuade and dissuade, include flattery and reproach, conditional threats and promises, appeals to reason and emotion, exempla, and various figures of speech (simile, metaphor, hyperbole, and personification) as well as the maxims, alternatives, and rhetorical questions examined above. Similarly worth investigating in Herodotean speeches and dialogues is what Lohmann has done with Homeric discourse: ring composition both within individual speeches and in dialogues as a whole; parallel composition between speeches. In content as well as in form, patterning provides evidence of the oral influence in composition.

In the narrative as in the discourse of the *Histories* it is possible to study oral features and to formulate an anatomy of oral composition. Important in the narrative flow are the direction statements, transitions by association sometimes simulating causation and sometimes introducing digressions that spiral forward and feed back into the consequently amplified account, insistence on forward movement, theme recurrence, and evidence of audience participation.

If, as seems likely from the presence in the *Histories* of such oral features as characterize both the Homeric epic and Herodotus' sources, the historian started reporting the results of his inquiries orally in lectures, there would undoubtedly have been audience reactions in the form of questions and objections. Thereafter, in subsequent re-creations of particular subjects Herodotus must not only have taken these reactions into account both with fuller explanations (witness the ubiquitous use of *gar*) and with background digressions but also gradually have compacted his wide-ranging and various material into the tightly constructed narrative that he finally wrote down. The homely but most telling image for this kind of composition, which alone can account for both virtues and defects of Homeric and Herodotean works, is that of making a snowman. At first, as one rolls individual parts, some clumps of snow, large or small, pack together in intimate cohesion, while others fall away of their own weight or incompatibility; then as one joins together the individual parts, sculpting and further fashioning are necessary to achieve a properly organic arrangement; and the whole is a product that combines growth and creation as only a work composed orally and over time with audience participation can do.

If Herodotus had been asked to comment on his method of composing the *Histories*, he might have been tempted to paraphrase Plato's still-to-be-written remark about the lover and the beloved (*Euthyphro* 14c):

ἀνάγκη γὰρ τὸν ἱστορέοντα τοῖς ἱστορημένοις ἀκολουθεῖν, ὅπῃ ἂν ἐκεῖνα ὑπάγῃ.

Appendixes
Notes
Selected Bibliography
Indexes

Appendix I

On Motivation

That Herodotus considered motivation important and a proper object of research is evident not only from the care with which he presents motives for the great majority of actions reported but also in his apparent need to offer alternatives in situations where he has either no information about motives or no clear preference between possibilities. Note, for example:

i.19.2. εἴτε δὴ συμβουλεύσαντός τευ, εἴτε καὶ αὐτῷ ἔδοξε

i.61.2. εἴτε ἱστορεύσῃ εἴτε καὶ οὔ, φράζει τῇ ἑωυτῆς μητρί

i.86.2. ἐν νόῳ ἔχων εἴτε δὴ ἀκροθίνια ταῦτα καταγιεῖν θεῶν ὅτεῳ δή, εἴτε καὶ εὐχὴν ἐπιτελέσαι θέλων, εἴτε καὶ πυθόμενος τὸν Κροῖσον εἶναι θεοσεβέα

i.191.1. εἴτε δὴ ὧν ἄλλος οἱ ἀπορέοντι ὑπεθήκατο, εἴτε καὶ αὐτὸς ἔμαθε τὸ ποιητέον οἱ ἦν

ii.181.1. εἴτε ἐπιθυμήσας Ἑλληνίδος γυναικός, εἴτε καὶ ἄλλως φιλότητος Κυρηναίων εἵνεκα

iii.33. ὁ Καμβύσης ἐξεμάνη, εἴτε δὴ διὰ τὸν Ἆπιν εἴτε καὶ ἄλλως, οἷα πολλὰ ἔωθε ἀνθρώπους κακὰ καταλαμβάνειν (more explanation than motivation)

iii.121.2. εἴτε ἐκ προνοίης . . . εἴτε καὶ συντυχίη τις τοιαύτη ἐπεγένετο

iv.147.4. προσχόντι δὲ εἴτε δὴ οἱ ἡ χώρη ἤρεσε, εἴτε καὶ ἄλλως ἠθέλησε ποιῆσαι τοῦτο

iv.164.4. εἴτε ἑκὼν εἴτε ἀέκων ἁμαρτὼν τοῦ χρησμοῦ

viii.54. εἴτε δὴ ὧν ὄψιν τινὰ ἰδὼν ἐνυπνίου . . . εἴτε καὶ ἐνθύμιόν οἱ ἐγένετο ἐμπρήσαντι τὸ ἱρόν

ix.5.2. εἴτε δὴ δεδεγμένος χρήματα παρὰ Μαρδονίου, εἴτε καὶ ταῦτά οἱ ἑάνδανε

ix.91.1. εἴτε κληδόνος εἵνεκεν θέλων πυθέσθαι εἴτε καὶ κατὰ συντυχίην θεοῦ ποιεῦντος

In other cases where whatever motives may have existed are rendered insignificant by the catastrophic results, Herodotus apparently preferred to invoke the *dei genesthai* formula, judging that "what was had to be" whatever the motivation might have been. The chief examples are:

i.8.2. Χρῆν γὰρ Κανδαύλῃ γενέσθαι κακῶς

ii.133.3. δεῖν γὰρ Αἴγυπτον κακοῦσθαι ἐπ᾽ ἔτεα πεντήκοντά τε καὶ ἑκατόν (oracle speaking)

ii.161.3. ἐπεὶ δέ οἱ ἔδεε κακῶς γενέσθαι
iv.79.1. ἐπείτε δὲ ἔδεέ οἱ κακῶς γενέσθαι
v.92d1. ἐδεῖ δὲ ἐκ τοῦ ᾿Ηετίωνος γόνου Κορίνθῳ κακὰ ἀναβλαστεῖν
vi.135.3. ἀλλὰ δεῖν γὰρ Μιλτιάδεα τελευτᾶν μὴ εὖ
ix.109.2. τῇ δὲ κακῶς γὰρ ἔδεε πανοικίῃ γενέσθαι

Similar to the *dei genesthai* formula and similarly related to Herodotus' concern with motivation is his readiness to divine purpose from result. Thus because Deioces gained supreme power through just judgments he must have been motivated to judge justly by his desire for power (i.96–97). And because the result of Cyrus' immolation of Croesus was rescue by Apollo, one at least of Cyrus' suggested purposes was to learn if because of his piety the god would save him (i.86–87). Somewhat different are the cases where the result follows from a kind of negative purpose, that is, a rejection of a warning, so that, after a fashion, Polycrates purposed his own crucifixion by rejecting his daughter's warning (iii.124–125). And Herodotus was careful to show Xerxes mixed in purpose as he heeded Artabanus' warning about the contemplated Greek expedition (vii.11–18), thus matching the mixed result (his defeat and survival). Cyrus' defeat and death, resulting from fixed purpose and rejected warning, provide a clear and unmixed contrast (i.201–214).

Herodotus' interest in and use of motivation is, from one point of view, simply a part of his penchant for explaining. Just as it is a rare page in the *Histories* that does not show at least two clauses with *gar* to explain statements, attitudes, results, etc., so there are few actions undertaken by individuals or groups which are not in some fashion motivated. Not only is it the business of one who inquires to get answers, among which explanations and motivations must always play an important part, but also the one whose habits of composition are oral is both accustomed to audience questions and eager to anticipate them with explanations. Answers of this sort include both "external" and "internal" motivations: either the impulse to act comes from outside or it arises from within, as the alternatives listed above in cases of uncertainty suggest. External motivations range from command through proposal, advice, and appeal to simple but impelling information, and they may be conveyed in direct speech, in indirect discourse, or in narrative reporting. Internal motivations are mostly of the desiring, wishing, and fearing sort (*epithumeo, boulomai, deido,* etc.) and are ordinarily simply reported. The two kinds of motivation fulfill Herodotus' need as both inveterate inquirer and audience-pacifier to find answers and explain, but the internal variety seems to be limited to this need while the external has another dimension. That is, Herodotus uses external motivation as a linking device between actions and as a kinetic factor in the unfolding of events; internal motivation, coming as it does from within, makes no direct connection with other actions or events and ordinarily is either introduced and linked to what precedes only temporally (e.g., i.24.1, 141.1, 201.1) or evoked by one of the external motivators (e.g., i.21.1, 107.2, 115.1).

The role played by commands, appeals, and advice in external motivation is clear. The manner in which they are presented, on the other hand, is less immediately obvious and seems to depend chiefly on the importance and nature of the action itself: direct speech to instigate action that is unexpected and uncharacteristic enough to require special impetus (e.g., i.69.2 appeal, 110.3 command, 124.2 advice); reported speech in order to point up without emphasizing an expected response, either positive or negative (i.24.3 command, 59.2 advice, 152.1 appeal); narrative report when the action taken or refused is so likely that the motivation may almost be taken for granted (i.30.1 command, 74.1 appeal, 80.2 advice).

The presentation of motivating information differs from that of commands, appeals, and advice in being more closely connected with transitions and the arrangement of material. Thus if knowledge of an event might have motivated a particular action, it is characteristic of Herodotus' style to make a transition by using some one of the learning-formulas to connect the two. The Persian fleet's great loss by storm is reported in its proper place in the Persian advance (vii.188–191) and news comes to the Greek fleet (vii.192) to motivate their celebration and thanksgiving. But then the continued advance of the Persians goes on to Thermopylae so that it is only in viii.6 that Herodotus comes back to the Persian fleet and their intention to attack the Greek fleet at Artemisium. Now in order to motivate the Greek willingness to face the Persians, they must learn again of the Persian losses, so in viii.8 he introduces Skyllias the diver as a deserter, who, like his doublet Ameinocles in vii.190, had profited hugely from the Persian wrecks. And it is from hearing Skyllias' report (viii.9) that the Greeks are moved to plan their strategy.

Different from this sort of forward-looking learning that motivates the action which moves the story forward is the backward-looking learning that motivates action taken previously but which has only now become relevant; for example, in viii.71, only when the Persian army is marching against the Peloponnesus does the previous Greek effort to prevent their entry become important; it is therefore inserted thus: "Everything possible had been contrived so that the barbarians might not invade by land. For as soon as the Peloponnesians learned that Leonidas' men had perished at Thermopylae they rushed to the Isthmus." And the work is then described.

These examples use simple reports of learning, but information conveyed by direct and indirect discourse also motivates. How Herodotus chose among these ways of providing information to instigate action should perhaps be considered. The "having learned" formula was useful where neither the source of the intelligence nor the manner of its conveyance was necessary or material. The use of a messenger or an announcement should then belong to situations where there might be a question about how the information was conveyed. Examples of both these formulas from the first four books of the *Histories* illustrate the difference in usage and show at the same time the way in which both are often used to make a transition from a description of an event or situation to the action motivated by knowledge of it.

i.19.2–21.1. Alyattes sent to Delphi, and we hear what the oracle had to say along with the messenger. Only then do the two men whose actions are to be affected by their knowledge hear; and in this case the two different formulas are used, one for each. Periander, as a Greek and resident of nearby Corinth, could be presumed simply to have heard, hence the *puthomenon* formula ("Periander the son of Cypselus and close friend of Thrasybulus tyrant of Miletus, having heard the oracle given to Alyattes, sent word of it to Thrasybulus . . ."). Alyattes, as the somewhat remote Lydian king who had sent to consult the oracle, would have had a formal report ("Alyattes, when the oracle was announced to him, immediately sent a herald to Miletus . . ."). The movement of the narrative is completely natural: it goes to Delphi for the oracle which emerges first as local Greek news and then as an answer to the foreign consultant; Herodotus' knowledge of how this happened is both explained and guaranteed by two interspersed mentions of his sources ("So much I know from the Delphians; the Milesians add the following").

i.56.1–69.1 and iii.17.2–25.1. In both these cases a king sends to find out about a foreign people: Croesus "inquiring who of the Greeks was most powerful so he might take them as allies" and Cambyses "sending spies to the

Ethiopians." Again, in both cases, the narrative proceeds to supply the information that was sent for, so that it may motivate action. There is a difference, however: the ethnography of Greece and the stories of Athenian tyranny and Spartan internal and foreign affairs are presented primarily as part of Herodotus' "inquiry" into the background of East-West conflict with Croesus' inquiry merely providing the pretext; but the exchange between Cambyses' spies and the Ethiopian king, although it does provide a kind of Ethiopian *logos*, is given primarily for its provocative effect on Cambyses. In consequence, the ways in which Croesus and Cambyses learn the results of their inquiries must be different. That Cambyses' spies should make a report of all that they saw and heard suits the situation perfectly ("When they announced these things, Cambyses was angered by them and immediately marched against the Ethiopians"). But it would be incongruous for the "historical" material in i.56.2–68 to be given as a report to Croesus, so the much vaguer formula is used ("Croesus, learning all these things, sent messengers to Sparta").

i.96 and ii.121e. Knowledge of Deioces' just judging, which resulted in people flocking to him from miles around, is represented as being spread naturally and informally by word of mouth ("People in the villages roundabout, hearing that Deioces was alone in judging according to the right, . . . came to him to be judged"). But knowledge of the theft of the thief's body had to be officially reported to Rhampsinitus, since it was he who had ordered it hung up and reactions to it observed. ("The king, when the theft of the corpse was announced to him, carried on terribly and . . ."). In both cases Herodotus has reported in advance both the situation that gave rise to the learning and the intentions behind it, so that the narrative movement is straightforward from purpose to result to effect of the knowledge thereof (Deioces' desire for tyranny—Deioces' just judgments—people's coming to depend on him; Rhampsinitus' intent to identify the thief—hung-up corpse not mourned but stolen—fury and more fantastic attempt to identify the second thief).

i.52 and ii.152.4. This pair presents a somewhat different contrast. When Croesus tested various oracles he accepted the answer from Delphi but was also impressed by that of the Amphiareion (i.49). Herodotus, having noted this and then gone on to list at some length Croesus' offerings to Delphi, uses the *puthomenos* formula to return to the Amphiareion dedications ("These he sent to Delphi, and to Amphiaraus, having learned of his excellence and suffering, he dedicated a gold shield"). In the other case Herodotus, having reported the oracle given to Psammetichus about vengeance coming when bronze men appeared from the sea, tells of the arrival of bronze-clad Ionian and Carian pirates, which only someone on the spot was in a position to come and announce to Psammetichus, hidden in the marshes, "that bronze men coming from the sea were ravaging the plain." Because the man in hiding was in no position simply to hear, such a specific reporter was necessary, while in the case of Croesus, the having-learned formula is sufficiently vague to serve merely as an echo of previously imparted information.

Many other examples of each formula exhibit the same differences: formal announcement most often following on an earlier command to find something out or being made by the one person who was in a position to get the information; the having-learned formula serving in situations where the transmission of information was so natural that there could be no question as to the source or manner or where Herodotus is simply reviewing a subject's reaction to information previously conveyed.

Information leading to action may also be presented either in single speeches (see Appendix II, Table 3) or in dialogues. The most frequent form of dialogues of this sort is that of question and answer, in which the messenger formula is, as it were, dramatized.

i.47. Croesus sent messengers to ask the oracles what he was doing; the directly quoted oracle describes the peculiar operation he was performing in order to test it. This information motivated his serious consultation.

i.66. The Spartans consulted Delphi about conquering all of Arcadia; the directly quoted oracle predicts ambiguously that they will have Tegea to dance in and a fine plain to measure. This information motivates their attack.

iii.14.9–10. Cambyses asks for an explanation of Psammenitus' unexpected response to various injuries; Psammenitus' answer provides a kind of insight that motivates Cambyses' change to clemency.

The more elaborate conveyance of information in these examples seems to be required by the greater complication of the situations. Croesus' faith in the Delphic oracle could not be so compellingly motivated if he merely learned or had announced to him that it was the most trustworthy; the ambiguity of the oracle given to the Spartans and motivating their disastrous expedition could be expressed only by direct quotation of the answer to their question; and Cambyses' compassion for Psammenitus could be motivated only by something as dramatic as the latter's just and pitiable response to adversity.

A longer dialogue may also be used to lead up to motivating information. One example by its almost mythical quality even demonstrates how prone are Herodotus and/or his sources to see knowledge as a spur to action: a hexad of indirectly quoted questions and answer about the Paeonians motivates Darius' order to Megabazus to round up the Paeonians (v.13–15). The oddity of Darius' desire to transplant the Paeonians needs the dramatic build-up of a dialogue. But the Paeonians' learning of this order, which motivates their mobilization for an attack by sea, needs rumor only and so requires only *puthomenoi*.

It is such transparent tales as the one about the Paeonian transplantation that alert us to Herodotus' concern with the kind of personal motivation that is useful from a narrative point of view rather than with historical causes. Take, for example, the changing "causes" of Croesus' expedition against Cyrus, which serve both to explain why a man like Croesus might undertake such a war and to introduce the particular forces that drove him. In i.46 the transition from the Atys story to the expedition is made by the somewhat mechanical "Afterwards Cyrus' usurpation of Astyages' rule and the growth of Persian power put an end to Croesus' grief." This *men* clause is followed by a *de* clause which serves as a direction-statement that points the way for the next forty chapters: "and it occurred to him to check, if he could, the growing Persian power before it became great." This leads to his testing of the oracles and the subsequent famous reply of the Delphic oracle assuring him that if he makes the expedition against the Persians he will destroy a great kingdom. After his second question and the oracle's reply about Greek allies with its long parenthesis on Athenian and Spartan history, the role of the oracle as *peitho* is resumed vis-à-vis the "tragic warning" of Sandanis in i.71.

In i.73 Croesus' motivation for the expedition is reviewed and now includes: (1) a desire to acquire more land (implicit in the i.46 motivation); (2) trust in the oracle (tying in the intervening chapters 47–72); (3) a desire to take vengeance on Cyrus on behalf of Astyages (introducing the following tale of Croesus' connection with Astyages that explains this desire). In i.75 these motivations are recombined in order finally to launch the expedition: "Croesus, blaming this (dethronement of Astyages) on Cyrus, sent to ask the oracle if he should march against the Persians."

This addition to and renewal of Croesus' motives has been viewed as "a change of priorities gradually taking place in Croesus' thinking" (Stahl, 31–32) as if Herodotus' narrative reflected a moment-by-moment description of Croesus' intentions! Or it has been thought to represent an attempt to include material from contradictory sources (von Fritz, I, 237–238). But surely the different motives are used to provide transition from one item of background material to another while keeping the illusion of forward-motion in the narrative. Learning by inquiry is again of primary importance, but here it is not so much that Croesus' learning of various matters motivates his actions as that the audience comes to understand his involvement by learning of the forces acting on him.

Analytic List
of Herodotean Speeches

SINGLE SPEECHES

Quoted Directly (92)

Motivating Speeches (52)

In 52 cases (see Table 1) the speech provides impetus for the action that follows. In 46 of these cases the resulting action is intended by the speaker. In the 6 exceptions it is the subject matter of the speech (or oracle) rather than the intent of the speaker that provides the impetus; these exceptions are starred in the table.

Explaining Speeches (33)

Less numerous than the single speeches that motivate action on the part of others but no less important a feature of the narrative are the single utterances that provide explanation for the actions or situation of the speaker himself. These speeches are of two general sorts: (1) those calling for action on the part of others with no resulting action being reported (see Table 2); and (2) those in which the speaker's concern is more with his own action or situation (see Table 3). In both these cases, if we may judge Herodotus' purpose in including these speeches from their effect on the narrative, it seems evident that they were designed to serve the same explanatory function as the motivating speeches but that what they explain is why and how the speakers, rather than those spoken to, behave as they do or take the positions that they take. The fact that Herodotus does not report the resulting action in those cases when the implication is that it occurred (i.199.3; ii.78; iv.158.3; vi.97.2; vii.53; viii.22.1–2; ix.18.3, 98.3) and

Table 1

Reference	Speaker(s)	Intent (and means)	Audience	Action to be motivated
i.60.5	Heralds	Command (reason)	Athenians	Reception of Peisistratus
i.68.2–3	Smith	*Announcement (information)	Lichas	Discovery of Orestes' bones
i.69.1–2	Messengers	Appeal (reason, promise)	Spartans	Alliance
i.85.4	Dumb son	Command	Persian	Preservation of Croesus
i.97.3	Some Medes	Proposal (reason, promise)	Other Medes	Establishment of monarchy
i.110.3	Harpagus	Command (purpose, threat)	Mitradates	Exposure of baby Cyrus
i.114.5	Artembares	Announcement (information)	Astyages	Vengeance for insult
i.116.2	Astyages	Announcement (promise)	Artembares	Artembares' departure
i.121	Astyages	Command (information, promise)	Cyrus	Cyrus' departure to Persia
i.124	Harpagus	Advice (information, reason, promise)	Cyrus	Persian revolt
i.125.2	Cyrus	Command	Persians	Working party
i.206	Tomyris	Advice (reason), proposal (choice)	Cyrus	Choice of battlefield
i.207	Croesus	Advice (warning, reasons)	Cyrus	Decision about battlefield
iii.1.4	Nitetis	*Announcement (information)	Cambyses	War on Egypt
iii.40.1–4	Amasis	Advice (reasons, purpose)	Polycrates	Interruption of prosperity
iii.50.3	Procles	Appeal (question)	Grandsons	Son's hostility to Periander
iii.120.3	Mitrobates	Announcement (taunt)	Oroetes	Attack on Polycrates
iii.122.3	Messenger	Proposal (reason, promise)	Polycrates	Visit to Oroetes

Table 1, continued

Reference	Speaker(s)	Intent (and means)	Audience	Action to be motivated
iii.127.2–3	Darius	Appeal (information, reason)	Persians	Disposal of Oroetes
iii.145.2–3	Charilaus	Proposal (taunt, promise)	Maeandrius	Betrayal of Persians
iii.151.2	Babylonian	Announcement (taunt, promise)	Zopyrus	Self-mutilation
iv.3.3–4	Scythian	Advice (reason, promise)	Scythians	Mastery of slaves
iv.79.4	Borysthenite	Proposal (reason)	Scythians	Spying on king in orgy
iv.80	Sitalces	Proposal (reason)	Octamasades	Peaceful exchange
iv.98.2–3	Darius	Command (reason, promise)	Ionians	Guarding of Danube bridge
iv.159.3	Oracle	Prediction (threat)	Greeks	Settlement in Cyrene
v.23.2–3	Megabazus	Advice (reproach, reason, purpose)	Darius	Control of Histiaeus
v.33.4	Aristagoras	*Announcement (taunt)	Megabates	Forewarning to Naxians
v.98.2	Messenger	Proposal (promise, reason)	Paeonians	Return home to Paeonia
vi.9.3–4	Persian	Appeal	Ionian ex-tyrants	Separation of cities from revolt
vi.11.2	Dionysius	Appeal (threat, promise)	Ionians	Training for battle
vi.12.3	Some Ionians	Appeal (reproach, reason)	Other Ionians	Cessation of training
vi.77.2	Oracle	*Prediction (threat)	Argives	Imitation of enemy signals
vi.85.2	Theasides	Advice (warning)	Aeginetans	Respect for Spartan king
vi.108.2–3	Spartans	Advice (reason)	Plataeans	Alliance with Athens
vi.109.3–6	Miltiades	Advice (threat, promise)	Callias	Vote for immediate battle

vii.5.2	Mardonius	Advice (reason, purpose)	Xerxes	Expedition against Greece
vii.150.2	Herald	Appeal (reason, promise)	Argives	Neutrality
vii.172.2–3	Thessalians	Appeal (threat, reason)	Isthmus congress	Military aid
vii.220.4	Oracle	*Prediction (threat, reason)	Spartans	Leonidas' self-sacrifice
viii.24.2	Herald	Announcement	Persian fleet	Viewing of battlefield
viii.60–62	Themistocles	Advice (reasons, purposes, threats, promises)	Eurybiades	Decision for battle at Salamis
viii.75.2–3	Sicinnus	Announcement (reason)	Persians	Nocturnal channel guard
viii.84.2	Voice	Appeal	Greeks	Beginning of battle
viii.109	Themistocles	Advice (reason)	Athenians	Abandoning pursuit
ix.9.2	Chileos	Advice (threat)	Spartans	Despatch of army
ix.12.2	Argive	*Announcement (information)	Mardonius	Departure from Attica
ix.17.4	Harmocydes	Appeal (reasons)	Phocians	Bravery under fire
ix.21.2	Megarians	Appeal (reason, threat)	Greek generals	Military aid
ix.60	Pausanias	Appeal (reason, promise)	Athenians	Military aid
ix.87.1–2	Timegenides	Advice (reason)	Thebans	Surrender of medizers
ix.116.3	Artayctes	Appeal (reason)	Xerxes	Granting of temple

Table 2

Reference	Speaker(s)	Intent (with means)	Person(s) addressed	What is called for	What is explained
i.141.2	Fluteplayer	Command (reason)	Fish	Cessation of dance	Fluteplayer's anger
i.199.3	Man	Command	Woman	Prostitution	Toss of coin
ii.78	Servant	Command (reason)	Banqueters	Enjoyment of life	Presentation of corpse-image
iii.65	Cambyses	Appeal (information, promise, threat)	Persian nobles	Vengeance	Cambyses' *pathei mathos*
iii.137.2–3	Persian envoys	Announcement (threats)	Crotoniates	Surrender of Democedes	Persian impotence
iv.133.2	Scythians	Advice (promise)	Ionians	Abandonment of bridge	Scythian strategy
iv.158.3	Libyans	Advice (reason)	Colonists	Location of settlement	Particular location
vi.97.2	Datis	Appeal (reason)	Delians	Delians' return home	Persian respect for Greek gods

			Persian nobles	Courage and victory	Persian respect for Greek army
vii.53.	Xerxes	Appeal (reason, promise)			
viii.22.1–2	Themistocles	Appeal (reason)	Ionians	Help or neutrality	Themistocles' cleverness
ix.7	Athenian messengers	Appeal (reason)	Spartan ephors	Military aid	Athenian situation
ix.18.3	Mardonius	Appeal (promise)	Phocian army	Military cooperation	Persian respect for valor
ix.48	Mardonius	Proposal (reason, taunt)	Spartan army	Battle	Persian arrogance
ix.89	Artabazus	Announcement; command (promise)	Thessalians	Reception of army	Artabazus' success in escaping
ix.98.3	Leotychidas	Appeal	Ionians	Help or neutrality	Historical pattern, see viii.22.1–2
ix.120.2	Artayctes	Proposal (promise)	Xanthippus	Freedom at a price	Artayctes' wickedness

Table 3

Reference	Speaker(s)	Intent (with means)	Person(s) addressed	Subject	What is explained
i.128.1	Astyages	Announcement (threat)	(Unnamed)	Revolt of Cyrus	Killing of priests and recruiting
i.214.5	Tomyris	Announcement (reason)	Head of Cyrus	Rewards of victory	Her treatment of Cyrus' head
iii.29.2	Cambyses	Announcement	Priests of Apis	Apis' godhead	Slaughter of priests
iii.83.2	Otanes	Proposal (reason)	Other six conspirators	Eschewal of kingship	Special position of Otanes' line
iii.139.3	Syloson	Announcement (promise)	Darius	Disposition of cloak	Syloson's position as benefactor
v.1.3	Paeonians	Announcement (reason)	Themselves	Time for offensive	The Paeonians' victory
vi.86a	Milesian	Appeal (reason)	Glaucus	Deposit of funds	Milesian's trust in Glaucus
vi.86b2	Glaucus	Announcement (reason)	Milesian's sons	Return of deposit	Glaucus' untrustworthiness

vi.107.4	Hippias	Announcement (reason)	Companions	Tooth-dream	His abandonment of claim to Attica
vii.13.2–3	Xerxes	Announcement (reason)	Persians	Renunciation of expedition	His change of mind
vii.35.2	Xerxes	Announcement (threat, reason)	Hellespont	Bad behavior of Hellespont	His flogging and fettering water
vii.56.2	Someone	Announcement (question)	Zeus	Persian expedition	Greek awe of Persian power
vii.168.3	Corcyreans	Announcement (reason)	Persians	Corcyrean neutrality	Corcyrean abstention from battle
viii.106.3	Hermotimus	Announcement (threat)	Panionius	Vengeance	Wholesale castration
viii.110.2–3	Themistocles' messenger	Announcement (promise)	Xerxes	Freedom from pursuit	Themistocles' foresight
ix.58	Mardonius	Announcement (taunt)	Aleuads	Spartan cowardice	Mardonius' overconfidence
ix.82.3	Pausanias	Announcement	Greek generals	Greek-Persian contrast	Persian folly

that he includes the motivating speech even when it was ineffective shows that in all the Class 1 cases his concern was with the speaker's intention and purpose more than with the outcome. In all the Class 2 "explaining" speeches the emphasis is as much on characterization of both men and situations as it is on giving motive power to the action or situation described. Since the speaker is also for the most part the one who acts or holds the initiative, his utterance is concerned not with motivating others but with giving expression to impulses that motivate from within.

Prefiguring Speeches (6)

A few of the single utterances (see Table 4) serve to explain neither why the speakers nor why those addressed acted as they did. Rather, they seem to have as their chief function both the prefiguring of disaster and the fixing of responsibility therefor. The speaker in each case delivers a warning or threat indicating the troubles that will come if the advice is not taken; in this way the coming disaster is prefigured. It is also justified, and the responsibility for it is fixed, through the heedlessness of the person(s) addressed, whose willful refusal to consider possible consequences invites the worst. This way of explaining the cause of a disaster is in its own way a form of motivation, since the negative reaction to the warning gives impetus to the unfavorable outcome, just as positive reactions to motivating speeches are exemplified in the resulting action. So we come full circle in analyzing the functions of single utterances: from motivation through explanation and back to motivation.

Exception (1)

Only one of the 92 single speeches does not fit these categories of motivation and explanation. It is an oracle that was given unsolicited (i.65.3). It is apparently incomplete, since some claim that the priestess went on to detail elements of the Spartan constitution; but even what is quoted, which gives special recognition to Lycurgus, might be thought of as giving impetus to his reform movement. Thus, even the single utterance that does not fit squarely into the categories of motivation and explanation exhibits some connection and similarities with examples so categorized.

Table 4

Reference	Speaker(s)	Intent (with means)	Person(s) addressed	Subject	What is justified and prefigured
i.71.2–4	Sandanis	Advice (warning)	Croesus	War with Persia	Croesus' defeat and loss of kingdom
i.212.2–3	Tomyris	Advice (threat)	Cyrus	Continuation of war	Cyrus' defeat and death
v.56.1	Dream	Command (promise)	Hipparchus	Things unendurable	Hipparchus' death
vii.12.2	Dream	Advice (threat)	Xerxes	Greek expedition	More violent threats
viii.20.2	Oracle	Advice (warning)	Euboeans	Enemy attack	Great sufferings
ix.2	Thebans	Advice (warning, promise)	Mardonius	Strategy	Mardonius' failure and death

Quoted Indirectly

There are in the *Histories* approximately 80–100 single speeches quoted indirectly, the number varying as the line between indirect quotation and narrative reporting shifts. Between obvious examples of indirect discourse on the one hand and almost equally clear examples of narrative communication on the other, there is a large gray area of uncertainty. The following passages from Book i will illustrate the difficulty:

Indirect Discourse
i.13.2. τοσόνδε μέντοι εἶπε ἡ Πυθίη, ὡς Ἡρακλείδῃσι τίσις ἥξει ἐς τὸν πέμπτον ἀπόγονον Γύγεω.
i.97.1. γνοὺς ὁ Δηιόκης ἐς ἑωυτὸν πᾶν ἀνακείμενον οὔτε κατίζειν ἔτι ἤθελε ἔνθα περ πρότερον προκατίζων ἐδίκαζε, οὔτ' ἔφη δικᾶν ἔτι. οὐ γάρ οἱ λυσιτελέειν τῶν ἑωυτοῦ ἐξημεληκότα τοῖσι πέλας δι' ἡμέρης δικάζειν.

Narrative Communication
i.13.1. συνέβησαν ἐς τὠυτὸ οἵ τε τοῦ Γύγεω στασιῶται καὶ οἱ λοιποὶ Λυδοί, ἢν μὲν [δὴ] τὸ χρηστήριον ἀνέλῃ μιν βασιλέα εἶναι Λυδῶν, τὸν δὲ βασιλεύειν, ἢν δὲ μή, ἀποδοῦναι ὀπίσω ἐς Ἡρακλείδας τὴν ἀρχήν. ἀνεῖλέ τε δὴ τὸ χρηστήριον καὶ ἐβασίλευσε οὕτω Γύγης.
i.34.2. τοῦτον δὴ ὦν τὸν Ἄτυν σημαίνει τῷ Κροίσῳ ὁ ὄνειρος, ὡς ἀπολέει μιν αἰχμῇ σιδηρέῃ βληθέντα.

Uncertain
i.44.2. περιημεκτέων δὲ τῇ συμφορῇ δεινῶς ἐκάλεε μὲν Δία καθάρσιον, μαρτυρόμενος τὰ ὑπὸ τοῦ ξείνου πεπονθὼς εἴη, ἐκάλεε δὲ ἐπίστιόν τε καὶ ἑταιρήιον, τὸν αὐτὸν τοῦτον ὀνομάζων θεόν, τὸν μὲν ἐπίστιον καλέων, διότι δὴ οἰκίοισι ὑποδεξάμενος τὸν ξεῖνον φονέα τοῦ παιδὸς ἐλάνθανε βόσκων, τὸν δὲ ἑταιρήιον, ὡς φύλακα συμπέμψας αὐτὸν εὑρήκοι πολεμιώτατον.
i.59.2. Χίλων δὲ ὁ Λακεδαιμόνιος παρατυχὼν καὶ θεησάμενος τὸ τέρας συνεβούλευε Ἱπποκράτεϊ πρῶτα μὲν γυναῖκα μὴ ἄγεσθαι τεκνοποιὸν ἐς τὰ οἰκία, εἰ δὲ τυγχάνει ἔχων, δεύτερα τὴν γυναῖκα ἐκπέμπειν, καὶ εἴ τίς οἱ τυγχάνει ἐὼν παῖς, τοῦτον ἀπείπασθαι.
i.80.3. παραίνεσε τῶν μὲν ἄλλων Λυδῶν μὴ φειδομένους κτείνειν πάντα τὸν ἐμποδὼν γινόμενον, Κροῖσον δὲ αὐτὸν μὴ κτείνειν, μηδὲ ἢν συλλαμβανόμενος ἀμύνηται.

Mixed Indirect and Narrative
i.78.3. Τελμησσέες μέντοι τάδε ἔγνωσαν, στρατὸν ἀλλόθροον προσδόκιμον εἶναι Κροίσῳ ἐπὶ τὴν χώρην, ἀπικόμενον δὲ τοῦτον καταστρέψεσθαι τοὺς ἐπιχωρίους, λέγοντες ὄφιν εἶναι γῆς παῖδα, ἵππον δὲ πολέμιόν τε καὶ ἐπήλυδα.

When we are dealing with dialogues it is somewhat easier to identify what might reasonably be called indirect speeches. That is, where patterns of question-and-answer, challenge-and-response, thesis-antithesis-synthesis, etc., are clearly defined by several examples in which all speeches are quoted directly, dialogues that exhibit the same pattern but are directly quoted only in part make it possible to consider as indirect speeches even those narrative communications that replace the direct speeches of the pattern. What are counted as indirect single speeches in the following list are the examples that are most similar in form and content to such parts of dialogues. The judgment has been necessarily subjective, and therefore no definite statistics can be based on this group. (The letters M, E, and P indicate Motivating, Explaining, and Prefiguring.)

i.13.2	oracle P		iv.95.3	announcement E
i.44.2	prayer E		iv.125.4	announcement E
i.59.2	advice P		iv.136.1	appeal M
i.78.3	announcement E		iv.142	announcement E
i.80.3	command M		iv.144.2	announcement E
i.87.1	prayer E		iv.147.3	announcement E
i.97.1	announcement E		iv.151.2	announcement E
i.127.2	announcement E		iv.162.2	announcement E
i.141.1–2	announcement E		v.1.2	oracle M
i.152.1	appeal E		v.29.1	announcement E
i.172.2	announcement E		v.29.2	announcement E
ii.55.2	command M		v.33.3	announcement E
ii.121a2	announcement E		v.36.3	advice E
iii.4.3	advice M		v.43	announcement M
iii.19.2	announcement E		v.67.2	appeal E
iii.30.2	announcement M		v.84.1	announcement E
iii.39.4	announcement E		v.87.2	question E
iii.43.2	announcement E		v.89.2	oracle M
iii.77.2	question E		v.97.1–2	announcement M
iii.118.2	announcement E		vi.29.2	announcement E
iii.130.4	question E		vi.37.1	advice M
iii.130.4	announcement E		vi.37.2	announcement E
iii.133.2	appeal M		vi.61.5	announcement P
iii.137.5	announcement E		vi.65.3	announcement E
iii.138.2	announcement E		vi.76.2	announcement E
iii.144.1	announcement E		vi.99.2	announcement E
iii.145.1	announcement E		vi.100.3	appeal M
iii.154.1	question E		vi.105.2	announcement M
iv.14.2	announcement E		vi.126.2	announcement M
iv.15.2	announcement E		vi.132	announcement M
iv.43.2–3	announcement E		vi.133.2	announcement E
iv.43.5–6	announcement E		vii.3.2–3	advice M

vii.6.4	announcement E	viii.112.1	announcement E
vii.120	advice E	viii.116.1	announcement E
vii.136.1	announcement E	viii.135.3	announcement E
vii.147.1	announcement E	ix.33.4	announcement E
vii.168.4	announcement E	ix.38.2	announcement E
vii.203	announcement E	ix.44.2	announcement M
vii.219.1	announcement E	ix.72.2	announcement E
vii.233.1	announcement E	ix.77.1	announcement E
viii.2.2	announcement E	ix.100.1	announcement E
viii.19.2	advice M	ix.107.1	announcement E
viii.81	advice M		

PAIRS OF SPEECHES*

Pairs of speeches, like singles, occur both in isolation and as parts of longer dialogues. Since, however, the analysis of long dialogues is not always simple and the definition of their component parts is not always clear, only independent pairs are used here to determine the content and function of paired speeches. After the independent pair is defined, pattern pairs in longer dialogues may be more easily recognized.

Paired speeches may be of three kinds: two speeches quoted directly; two speeches quoted indirectly; a pair of which one speech is quoted directly and one indirectly. As with single speeches, the directly quoted examples should provide the standard. Of these there are 33 examples; the number of speeches is therefore 66. The number of patterns is six.

Pair Pattern One: Motivation by Command, Appeal, or Advice, with Affirmative Response

Some actions are too complex to be motivated by straightforward command, appeal, or advice. The simple impetus for action needs to be amended, conditioned, or revised in some way in order to provide the proper motivation. In these cases a pair of speeches is required: the first is very like the single speeches of command, appeal, or

---

*In the dialogues listed in this section and the following sections of Appendix II, one or even two of the "speeches" are not so much indirectly quoted as reported in narrative form; but because the dialogues conform to the patterns of pair, triad, etc., in every other respect, they are included under the appropriate rubric.

advice; the second is a partial agreement expressed in such a way as to condition, explain, or set the scene for subsequent action.

i.36. The Mysians' request for Croesus' son and hunters to kill a boar motivates the hunt, but without Croesus' refusal to let his son participate there is no motivation for the son's objection, which finally leads to Croesus' agreement and a different unsuccessful effort to save the boy.

i.41–42. Croesus' appeal to Adrastus motivates Adrastus' escort of his son, but without Adrastus' statement that a man dogged by misfortune has no place in sporting expeditions we would not be prepared for his fatal spearthrow.

i.108.4–5. Astyages' command that the baby be killed motivates the killing, but without Harpagus' carefully ambiguous response that does not commit him to acting in his own person there would be no lead-in to his turning over the murder to Mitradates.

iv.97.2–6. Coes' advice motivates the holding of the Danube bridge, but without Darius' acknowledgement of his debt to Coes for the advice the scene would not be set for his later generous repayment (v.11).

iv.136–139. The Scythians' command to the Ionians to abandon the bridge motivates the partial break-up, but without Histiaeus' seeming acceptance and encouragement of the Scythians in their pursuit of the Persians there would be no motivation for their departure.

v.31. Aristagoras' appeal for a fleet to take Naxos motivates the Persian expedition, but without Artaphernes' insistence on doubling the size of the fleet the magnitude of the undertaking would not have been motivated.

In all these cases a single speech of command, appeal, or advice could have been used, but the result would have been a flat narrative lacking in the nexus of interaction that gives both depth and continuity. The sense of the onward march of events is achieved by a combination of backcasting, by which future events cast their shadows before, and forecasting or prefiguring. In these particular cases of paired-speech motivation, secondary uses of the pattern show added functions:

i.209–210. Cyrus' command to have Darius put under guard until his return and Hystaspes' conditional acceptance follow the pattern, but what is motivated and conditioned by the two speeches is irrelevant and immaterial to the narrative. The real purposes served are the demonstration of Cyrus' heedlessness of warnings and the prediction of Darius' eventual succession to the throne. The use of a paired-speech pattern for this purpose suggests how convenient and habitual such patterns must have been.

ix.76. The Coan lady's appeal for rescue and Pausanias' judicious and restrained answer follow the pattern, but what is motivated and explained by the two speeches is not so important as the demonstration of Pausanias' anti-tyrannic behavior. (Cf. iii.80.5, *biatai gunaikas*.)

Thus Pair Pattern One appears in situations in which the motivation for an action (or the demonstration of a characteristic) is not single and straightforward but a combination of instigation and amendment.

Pair Pattern Two: Explanation by Command, Appeal, or Advice, with Negative Response

Some explanations also require a pair of speeches rather than a single utterance. But here it is not the nature of subsequent action that determines the use of two speeches; it is the situation itself which, because it does not naturally give rise to an explanatory speech, requires another speech evoking that explanation. That is, unless a particular course of action is recommended, an explanation of why it is rejected does not arise naturally.

ii.173. The Egyptians' advice to Amasis to act with more dignity is rejected with an explanation and justification of his behavior.

iii.142.3–5. Maeandrius' appeal for six talents and a priesthood in exchange for the Samian rule left him by Polycrates is rejected in such a way as to explain his imprisonment of the nobles and to justify, after a fashion, their subsequent slaughter.

vii.135. Hydarnes' advice to submit is rejected by the Greek heralds with an explanation and justification of their intransigent attitude toward Darius.

viii.59. Themistocles' rejection of Adeimantus' stricture or advice ("Those who start too soon in the races are punished." "And those who are left behind are not crowned") explains his position in the forefront of action and planning.

ix.78–79. Pausanias' rejection of Lampon's advice to mistreat Mardonius' corpse explains and justifies not only his but also the Greeks' moderation and decency.

In these cases the speech of appeal or advice serves not to motivate an action but rather to provoke an explanation of why that action is not taken.

Pair Pattern Three: Prefiguration by Command, Appeal, or Advice, with Negative Response

A pair of speeches rather than a single speech is used also to prefigure disaster when there is explicit rejection of positive advice or command rather than simple failure to heed a negative warning. That is, the future failure of a person undertaking action can be prepared for with one speech of warning to which he pays no attention; but if his failure is to result from his refusal to take a recommended action, two speeches are required.

iii.36.1–3. Cambyses' rejection of Croesus' advice to behave more moderately not only explains his effort to kill Croesus but also, by characterizing his irrationality, prefigures and helps to justify his final fate.

v.72.3. Cleomenes' refusal to heed the priestess' command to go out of the shrine justifies his failure to take the acropolis.

viii.114. Xerxes' rejection of the herald's appeal for recompense for Leonidas' death by turning it over to Mardonius provides ironic explanation and justification of Mardonius' subsequent payment with his life.

Pair Pattern Four: Motivation by Question and Answer

Other pairs of speeches in which the first one serves to evoke the second are made up of question and answer. In some of these pairs the second speech motivates action in much the save way as single speeches of announcement do. The difference lies in the fact that in some situations the motivating speech does not arise naturally but has to be evoked.

i.155. Only in answer to Cyrus' question as to where the Lydian troubles will end can Croesus suggest a solution that motivates Cyrus' action.

ii.114. Only in answer to Thonis' question about the treatment of Paris can Proteus give his order motivating the following action.

iii.14.9–10. Only in response to Cambyses' question about his unexpected reaction to family sorrows and those outside can Psammenitus make the statement that motivates Cambyses' clemency.

iv.9.3–5. Only in answer to the nymph's question as to what to do with the sons she says she has conceived can Heracles give the orders that motivate her actions.

v.79.2–80. Only in answer to the assembly's query as to what else the oracle could mean can one Theban hit upon the less obvious meaning of the "nearest" and so motivate the appeal to Aegina.

v.106. Only after Darius asked how the Ionians could revolt without Histiaeus' knowledge can he justify himself and make the appeal that moves Darius to let him return to Ionia.

Pair Pattern Five: Explanation by Question and Answer

Like the previous patterned pair, this has as its effective speech the second, which comes as the answer to a question and so is motivated by the first speech. Its effectiveness and function is the explanation and interpretation of past actions or present states of mind rather than the motivation of future actions.

i.87.3–4. Only in answer to Cyrus' question as to why he had invaded Persia can Croesus assert his belief in the folly of war while he blames the god.

i.109. Only in response to a natural wifely question about what he will do can Harpagus give expression to the inner debate that explains his quandary.

i.115. Only in answer to Astyages' accusing question about what he thought he was doing can the boy Cyrus explain his actions and justify them.

iv.126–127. Only in answer to Darius' question about what the Scythians were doing can Idanthyrsus explain Scythian tactics.

v.109. Only in response to the question where they wished to fight can the Ionian generals make a point of their proper mission.

v.111. Only in response to Onesilus' question whether he wishes to oppose Artybius or his horse can the groom explain his proper function as he chooses the horse.

vi.68–69. Only after Demaratus asks his mother what was the true story of his birth can she explain and justify her past actions.

Pair Pattern Six: Mixed Explanation and Motivation by Announcement Evoking Announcement

Single-speech announcements were seen to explain or motivate actions where those announcements arose naturally from the situation. When the motivating or explaining announcement can come only as a reaction to a previous declaration, this pair pattern is used.

iii.3. Only in answer to Cassandane's complaint about the Egyptian concubine can the boy Cambyses assert that he will turn Egypt upside down, thus both explaining and motivating the Egyptian expedition.

iii.42. Only in answer to the fisherman's graceful presentation of the fish to Polycrates can the latter be expected to issue an invitation to dinner, thus explaining and motivating the opening up of the fish.

viii.79–80. Without Aristides' announcement that the Greek position is surrounded there would be no reason for Themistocles to point out his (Aristides') greater credibility as he requests that he (Aristides) make the report.

ix.26–27. The Tegeates' statement of their claim to the position of honor evokes the Athenian counterclaim, which in turn explains the outcome.

MIXED PAIRS OF SPEECHES

In addition to Herodotus' directly quoted pairs of speeches there are 26 pairs in which one speech is quoted directly and the other indirectly. Of these pairs, 13 are made up of directly quoted oracles (3 in prose) that respond to indirectly quoted questions or narrative reports of consultation. The oracles regularly provide either explanations (Pair Pattern Five: i.47. 55, 66.1–2, 85.1–2, 90–91; iii.57.3–4; iv.163; v.92b2, 92e; vi.19) or negative motivation (Pair Pattern Four: i.174; iv.157.1–2; vii.169).

These 13 mixed pairs involving oracles belong to the same patterns as those directly quoted pairs in which the first speech serves to evoke the second, while the second provides motivation or explanation. Where the question is asked of one person by another, the more or less equal status of the speakers and the equality of their interaction are reflected in the use of direct quotation of question as well as answer. Where, however, the voice of the questioner is human and that of the respondent is divine, the comparative unimportance of the former is reflected in the less vivid reporting of the question.

The other 13 mixed pairs are more various. There is only one appeal (quoted indirectly) that is accepted (in direct quotation) with amendment so as to motivate action (Pair Pattern One: v.30.3–5), but there are 5 examples of appeal or advice (quoted directly) that are rejected (in indirect discourse) in such a way as to illuminate something past or explain something to come (Pair Pattern Two: iii.52.3–6; viii.29–30; ix.122; iii.53; vi.106). If the relative importance of the two speeches is reflected in the way they are quoted, we must assume that in the motivating pair the amendment is more important than the original appeal and that in the explaining pairs the appeal or advice is more important than the rejection. The latter assumption seems unlikely, so it is necessary to suggest another reason for the greater vividness and detail given to the appeal or advice by direct quotation. It may well be that we should look for this to the early development of Greek rhetoric, in which formulas of persuasion must have received most of the attention from earliest times. Furthermore, the kinds of argumentation *for* a particular action are likely to be more general and interchangeable from one situation to another than the bases for rejection, which must, from the speaker's point of view, be specific, and which ought, from the historian's point of view, to illuminate the context. This hypothesis will be tested with other mixed dialogues and examined in detail in Appendix IV, Direct and Indirect Discourse.

In addition to the 6 pairs involving appeal or advice, there are 7 mixed pairs made up of announcements and responses. In 4 (i.45; vi.63.2; viii.5.2, 125) the announcement is indirectly quoted and the response is given directly; in three the form of quotation is reversed (i.62–63; ii.181; vii.136.2). Is it possible to suggest a reason for the changing form of quotation that will fit all these cases? In the group of 4 with directly quoted responses, it is clear that all share a dramatic "punchline" quality: i.45, Croesus' unexpected forgiveness of Adrastus; vi.63, Ariston's disclaimer of paternity; viii.5, Themistocles' calling Adeimantus' bluff with a bigger bribe; viii.125, Themistocles' turning Timodemus' insult back on its author. Does this apply in reverse to the 3 with indirectly quoted responses? The answer is affirmative for i.62–63: Peisistratus' colorless response to Amphilytus' poetic prophecy. This may also be true of ii.181, where the concubine's prayer for Amasis' potency pales by comparison with his threatening announcement. But for vii.136.2, where Xerxes refuses to accept the heralds' offer of themselves as reparation for slain Persian heralds, the situation at first glance seems to be identical with that of i.45, where Croesus refuses to accept Adrastus' offer of himself. There is, however, a difference in that although Adrastus was technically guilty, Croesus holds a god responsible, while the actual guiltlessness of the heralds makes Xerxes' refusal to let them take the responsibility seem more natural than striking.

As far as function is concerned, the responses to announcements in these 7 mixed pairs do not, like those of the comparable directly quoted pairs (Pair Pattern Six), so much explain the context as counter the effects of the announcement and make it null and void.

INDIRECTLY QUOTED PAIRS

In addition to directly quoted pairs of speeches and mixed pairs there are many pairs that are indirectly quoted in their entirety. Here, as with indirectly quoted single speeches, there is a difficulty of definition. The present count, therefore, is highly subjective, including some pairs in which the speeches are perhaps more reported than indirectly quoted and excluding others of much the same sort. The present sample of 51 includes 32 of the question-and-answer variety, 16 involving appeals, advice, or announcement and response, and 3 made up of parallel claims or proposals. Of the 32 question-and-answer pairs more than half involve consultation of an oracle with the answer serving most often to authorize or motivate action but occasionally to prevent it (Pair Pattern Four)* and only once to validate a claim (Pair Pattern Five: whether Demaratus was the son of Ariston; vi.66). The other question-and-answer pairs provide information that either moves someone to action (Pair Pattern Four: i.24.7; ii.121e4; iii.32.2; iv.9.2; v.92eta2; vii.218) or explains a situation or the reactions to it (Pair Pattern Five: i.122; ii.118.3; iii.31.2–3; iv.143; v.124–125; vi.3, 67.2–3; vii.37, 151). The 16 examples of appeal, advice, or announcement all meet with negative response: announcements are countered (Pair Pattern Six: ii.18; iii.135.2–3; iv.149.1; vi.82; vii.226; viii.90, 111); appeal and advice are rejected (Pair Pattern Two: ii.30; iii.58.3; iv.84.1; v.84.2, 103.1; vii.168.1; viii.61, 108; ix.117). In the 3 pairs that present parallel claims or proposals, both are rejected (Pair Pattern Two: i.82.6, 170; vi.68.2). In general these indirectly quoted exchanges serve to illustrate and explain situations by reflecting the kind of conflict that gave rise to them. Many of the situations thus marked by these exchanges are somewhat off the main line of the narrative; this and the comparative brevity of the speeches may explain the use of indirect quotation rather than direct.

This brief survey of paired speeches shows that in form, content, and function they divide into two large groups. The first includes those in which the first speech is like one of the single-speech types; it is answered by a second speech of a sort not found among single speeches. That is, commands, appeals, and advice are amended in order to motivate or rejected in order to explain, while announcements are countered, also to explain. The second group includes those pairs in which the second speech is the same as one of the single-

---

*Authorization ordinarily follows a question about a particular course of action—whether to adopt names of gods (ii.52.2–3); whether to obey an apparition (iv.15.3); whether Dorieus will take the land he attacks (v.43); whether Miltiades should go with the Dolonci (vi.35.3–36). Positive motivation usually results from more open-ended questions asking what to do about something or how to cope with something: Alyattes' illness (i.19.2); Theran drought (iv.151.1); Theran troubles (iv.156.1–2); Cyrenaean troubles (iv.161.1–2); vengeance on Athens (v.79.1); honeycombed head (v.114.2); Apsinthian war (vi.34); Persian invasion (vii.178); adequacy of thank-offerings (viii.122); offspring (ix.33.2). Negative motivation follows questions that should not have been asked: whether to evict Adrastus from Sicyon (v.67.2); whether to bury or remove the treasures from Delphi (implying that the god can not take care of his own) (viii.36.1).

speech types; it is evoked by a first speech of a sort not found among single speeches; that is, questions evoke either commands, appeals, advice, and announcements that motivate, or they call forth justifications, announcements, and predictions that explain. In other words, pairs of speeches are used where a single-speech type (command, appeal, advice, announcement) needs to be evoked by a first speech, or where such a single-speech type must be either modified or rejected by a second speech. Generally, and as might be expected, pairs occur in situations where two points of view are represented so that they are more often useful in explaining situations of conflict, but they may also serve to motivate compounded or complex actions.

TRIADS

Of the 26 independent three-speech dialogues in Herodotus' *Histories*, 17 follow a pattern of question, answer, and conclusion or synthesis; the other 9 are somewhat more various but can be generally defined as including challenge, response, and conclusion or synthesis. In the large majority of cases (20) there are only two speakers (*aba*), and the first speaker draws a conclusion in the third speech on the basis of the second speaker's response to the first speech. Where there are three speakers, it should be noted that the third speech is not only "synthetic" in putting together the first two but also antithetic to the second speech in providing a different response. In the individual examples of the two patterns below, the way in which the speeches are quoted by Herodotus will be indicated as follows: upper case initials of the appropriate pattern for directly quoted speeches; lower case initials for those indirectly quoted; and lower case in parentheses for a simple report of communication. That is, qAS indicates that the question is in indirect discourse while answer and synthesis are directly quoted; C(r)S indicates that challenge and synthesis are direct while the response is merely noted.

Triad Pattern One: Question-Answer-Synthesis (17)

i.35 QAS (explaining Adrastus' presence and debt to Croesus)
Croesus: Who are you and whence? Whom did you kill?

Adrastus: I am Adrastus and I murdered my brother.
Croesus: You have come to friends and must bear up.

i.117–118 QAS (motivating dinner-visit, but really explaining set-up for revenge)
Astyages: What happened to the child?
Harpagus: I ordered the cow-herd to kill it and sent a trusty servant to see it had been done.
Astyages: (having told the story) Send your boy to welcome him and come to dinner to celebrate.

i.126.3–6 qaS (motivating Persian revolt)
Cyrus asked whether the feast or the previous day's toil was preferable.
Persians said the difference was great, between all good and all bad.
Cyrus: Revolt with me and you shall have all these goods and many more.

iii.32.3–4 qaS (elaborating and characterizing)
Sister-wife asked which lettuce he preferred.
Cambyses said the leafy one rather than the plucked one.
Sister-wife: And yet you imitated the other, stripping the house of Cyrus.

iii.34.4–5 qaS (explaining background of Cambyses' later remarks)
Cambyses asked how he was in relation to his father.
Persians said he was the better man.
Croesus: Not so good since you have no son such as he had.

iii.64 qaS (explaining location of Cambyses' death)
Cambyses asked what the name of the city was.
They said it was Ecbatana.
Cambyses: Here it is fated that Cambyses will die.

iii.78 qAS (motivating Darius' death-stroke, but really elaborating and characterizing)
Gobryas asked why he did not strike the magus.
Darius: For fear that I might hit you.
Gobryas: Use your sword, even through both of us.

iv.150 qaS (motivating choice of Battus)
Grinnus asked about other things.
Oracle told him to found a colony in Libya.
Grinnus: I am too old; bid one of the younger men to do this.

vi.1 qaS (elaborating and characterizing)
Artaphernes asked why it seemed best for the Ionians to revolt.
Histiaeus said he knew nothing of the matter.
Artaphernes: You sewed the shoe and Aristagoras put it on.

vi.80 qaS (explaining failure to take Argos)
Cleomenes asked what god the grove belonged to.

A deserter said it was the grove of Argos.
Cleomenes: O Apollo, how you deceived me saying I would take Argos.*

vii.128–130   qAS (explaining Thessalian medism)
Xerxes asked if it was possible for the river to reach the sea by another channel.
Guides: This is the only exit.
Xerxes: The Thessalians are wise to surrender knowing how easily their country could be flooded.

vii.147.3   qAS (elaborating and characterizing)
Xerxes asked where the ships were going.
Counselors: To your enemy, carrying grain.
Xerxes: Are we not going there too? How do they do wrong carrying grain for us?

viii.57   q(a)S (explaining and motivating Themistocles' visit to Eurybiades)
Mnesiphilus asked what had been planned.
(He learned that it had been agreed to retreat and fight at the Isthmus.)
Mnesiphilus: If they leave here, you will never fight for a united fatherland.

viii.65   qAS (elaborating and characterizing)
Demaratus asked what the sound was.
Dicaeus: This must be divine and so portends great harm to the king.
Demaratus: Do not tell anyone or you will lose your head.

viii.67–68   qaS (prefiguring Xerxes' defeat at Salamis)
Mardonius asked whether Xerxes should plan to fight a sea-battle.
The generals all said he should.
Artemisia: You have already done all you set out to do; a battle will be dangerous.

viii.118   qAS (elaborating and characterizing)
Xerxes asked if there was any chance of salvation.
Pilot: None, unless we have fewer passengers.
Xerxes: Now you nobles can show your care for my safety by jumping overboard.

ix.42   q(a)S (elaborating and characterizing)
Mardonius asked if anyone knew of a prophecy about a Persian defeat.
(No one answered, either from ignorance or fear.)
Mardonius: I know one but it cannot operate since we did not sack Delphi.

Some general remarks about form, content, and function may be made about this comparatively homogeneous group. The first and

*Disregard of grammar on the part of either the oracle or Cleomenes is troublesome; if the oracle used *Argos* as an accusative object of a verb, Cleomenes had every right to take it as the neuter third-declension name of the City and should not now confuse it with the masculine second-declension name of the hero. The only possibility is that the oracle used a passive construction and omitted the article: Argos will be taken.

third speakers in these triads are invariably individuals; only in the second speech, which supplies the information that is reacted to, are there plural or anonymous speakers. Both the group nature and the anonymity of the answerer seem to indicate the comparative unimportance of that role, in some situations at least. This de-emphasis is witnessed also by the frequency with which the answer is quoted indirectly (8 of 17) or merely reported as conveying information (2). Although the questioner is quoted indirectly still more frequently, he is invariably given a directly quoted third speech, except in the 2 cases where there are three speakers. These 2 dialogues (iii.34.4–5 and viii.67–68) are in form almost a link between pair and triad; like a pair they consist only of question and answer, but because there are two answers, of which the second reacts to the first, they are more like a triad. These 2 might be called an inflated pair, while the other 15 appear to be not so much a combination of pair and single as two overlapping pairs, with the second speech serving both to answer the first and evoke the second. The two overlapping pairs thus combine the pair pattern of question and answer with that of announcement and response, with the second speech being both answer and announcement. This answer-announcement speech is of the same type as many single speeches, while the question-speech has many parallels in pairs; the reaction or synthesis-speech has some of the same characteristics as single speeches of announcement, command, or advice, but by virtue of its position and relation with the two preceding speeches it has more the nature of a conclusion, and sometimes of a punchline.

It follows then that the kind of situation that calls for a triadic dialogue is one where the information, reasoning, or decision on which a conclusion is based can best be introduced by a question asking for it. The purpose served by triads is most often either explaining or elaborating and characterizing. Motivation is comparatively unimportant and plays a primary role only in i.126.3–6. The one case of prefiguring features a third speech that is most like the unheeded single speeches of warning. Generally speaking, the question-answer-synthesis triad is more often an embellishment of the narrative than it is essential to it. Characters appear more vivid, situations are seen more clearly, and the mechanics of human reason are presented more convincingly by means of these triads, but both narrative and history could function adequately without them.

In 10 of the triads the question is a request for information (i.35, 117–118; iii.64; vi.80; vii.128–130, 147; viii.57, 65, 118; ix.42); in 5 the request is for an opinion or decision (i.126; iii.32, 34.4–5; iv.150; viii.67–68); in 2 it is for an explanation or reason (iii.78; vi.1). But whether information, opinion, or reason was requested and given, the conclusion is regularly either a recommendation (i.35, 117–118, 126; iii.78; iv.150; viii.65, 118) or a realization (iii.32, 34.4–5, 64; vi.1, 80; vii.128–130, 147; viii.57, 67–68; ix.42).

Triad Pattern Two: Challenge-Response-Synthesis (9)

i.53 cQa (command, question, answer; perhaps not a true triad; prefiguring disaster and motivating alliance)
Croesus told Lydians what they were to ask.
Lydians: Croesus asks if he should campaign and if he should take an ally.
Oracle said he would destroy a great kingdom, and to take the strongest.

i.164 crs (proposal, counterproposal, conclusion; explaining Phocaean getaway)
Harpagus said he would be satisfied if they destroyed one tower, etc.
Phocaeans said they wanted one day of no siege to consider.
Harpagus said he knew what they would do, but he would let them consider.

ii.133 crs (announcement, counterannouncement, conclusion; explaining Mycerinus' regimen)
Oracle said he would have only six years to live.
Mycerinus objected that his piety deserved better reward.
Oracle said it was because his piety defied fate.

iii.80–82 CRS (proposal, counterproposal, conclusion; explaining Persian monarchy)
Otanes: Monarchy is bad; democracy is good.
Megabyzus: Democracy is as bad as monarchy; aristocracy is good.
Darius: Neither democracy nor aristocracy can be as good as monarchy.

iv.118–119 C(r)S (appeal, acceptance, rejection; explaining Scythian tactics of leading Persians to their neighbors)
Scythians: We need your help, or you will be next.
(Some chiefs agreed to help.)
Other chiefs: You started this and can take your punishment; we are not involved.

v.91–93 CRs (appeal, rejection, conclusion; explaining Athenian freedom from tyranny and prefiguring Athenian-Corinthian rivalry)
Spartans: Help us to restore Hippias as tyrant in Athens.

Corinthian: We cannot support despotism, since it produces terrible results (with example).
Hippias predicted that Corinth would regret leaving Athens free.

vi.86   crS (appeal, rejection, conclusion: explaining Aeginetan resumption of hostilities with Athens)
Leotychidas asked for return of Aeginetan hostages.
Athenians refused, saying they would not yield them unless both kings asked.
Leotychidas: Not returning deposits is impious and can be dangerous (with example).

vi.139   crS (announcement, counterannouncement, conclusion: explaining Athenian possession of Lemnos)
Pelasgians said they were willing to pay the penalty for the crime.
Athenians said they wanted Lemnos on a silver platter.
Pelasgians: You may have it when a ship sails there from Attica on a north wind.

viii.94   C(r)s (announcement, rejection, conclusion: explaining and motivating Corinthian fleet's return to battle)
Men on *keles:* You are betraying Greeks, who are winning.
(Adeimantus disbelieved.)
Men on *keles* insisted that they might be taken hostage as proof.

One triad (iv.118–119) is of the inflated-pair variety, with both acceptance and rejection of the appeal. Additionally, both the first and the last may not be true triads at all. Not only do both of them motivate action as well as either explain or prefigure, but also one of them (i.53) neglects the unities of time and place, and the other (viii.94) has no real second speech. The remaining 6 are all composed of overlapping pairs, with the second speech both countering or rejecting the first and evoking the third. Where there are only two speakers, the third speech is the first speaker's reaction (in the form of revision or expansion) to the objection made by the second speaker (i.164; ii.133; vi.86, 139); where there are three speakers, the third one counters the second but also ties back to the first, either countering it too (iii.80–82) or seconding it from a different point of view (v.91–93). In all 6 cases, and in the inflated-pair triad as well (iv.118–119), the function is to provide a background that gives point to a state or action: background for the Phocaean escape, for Mycerinus' life-style, for the Persian reestablishment of monarchy, for Scythian tactics, for the renewed Aeginetan attack on Athens, and for the Athenian seizure of Lemnos. They do not motivate or explain why so much as they explain how the thing could be so and what factors were involved. That is, like the 17 question-answer-synthesis triads, they mostly elaborate and characterize; they are more an embellishment of the narrative than essential to it. These 9 are mostly longer and include more arguments and rhetorical devices, with the result that they serve both as a commentary on the action and an interpretation of the considerations important to the people involved.

TETRADS

Of the 47 independent tetrads, 29 comprise two-stage pairs, 9 show chiastic pairs, and 9 are miscellaneous. As indicated above (pp. 26–28), the two-stage pairs may be divided into three groups in accordance with the nature of the need for the second pair. In the first group it is the obscurity of the first response that evokes the second question or challenge; in the second group the first response is unsatisfactory or wrong; and in the third group the first response is incomplete or inadequate. Since several examples of each are outlined in the text, they are not repeated here except as references.

Two-stage Pairs (29)

First Response Obscure (8)

     i.67; iii.119; vii.209 (see pp. 27, 29)

     ii.162 crcr
c1 Patarbemis summoned Amasis.
r1 Amasis broke wind and told him to take that back.
c2 Patarbemis urged him to come.
r2 Amasis said he would arrive sooner than expected.

     iii.155 qAQA
q1 Darius asked who mutilated him and why.
A1 Zopyrus: I myself did, to win victory for the Persians.
Q2 Darius: How is this possible?
A2 Zopyrus: (Explanation.)

     iv.155 (q)AQ(a)
(q1 Battus asked about his voice.)
A1 Oracle: Apollo sends you as colonist to Libya.
Q2 Battus: I came about my voice; how can I settle Libya?
(a2 The oracle answered as before.)

v.92z q(a)q(a)
q1 Periander sent to ask how most safely to control the city.
(a1 Thrasyboulos took the messenger into a field and lopped off the tallest ears.)
q2 Periander inquired what advice had been given.
(a2 Messenger reported how insanely Thrasyboulos had behaved, but Periander understood.)

ix.11 Crq(a)
C1 Messengers: You will be sorry when Athens is conquered and joins Persia.
r1 Ephors said that troops were already on their way against the Persians.
q2 Messengers asked the meaning of this.
(a2 Ephors explained so that the messengers understood.)

First Response Unsatisfactory or Wrong (10)

i.116; iii.46; vi.129–130 (see pp. 27–28)

i.8–9 CRC(r)
C1 Candaules: You must see her naked.
R1 Gyges: I could not and should not.
C2 Candaules: Do not be afraid; you can do it this way.
(r2 Gyges could not escape and so he agreed.)

iii.51 qaqa
q1 Periander asked his older son what Procles had said.
a1 The boy told other things but did not remember Procles' parting shot.
q2 Periander insisted there must have been something else.
a2 The boy finally said it.

iii.130.1–2 q(a)(q)a
q1 Darius asked if he knew medicine.
(a1 Democedes denied all knowledge.)
(q2 Darius threatened him, asking for the truth.)
a2 Democedes admitted some knowledge.

v.39–40 CrC(r)
C1 Ephors: Let your wife go and get another.
r1 Anaxandrides said he would do neither. (Cf. ix.111 below.)
C2 Ephors: Well, keep the one and add another.
(r2 Anaxandrides agreed.)

vi.69.2 qa(c)r
q1 My husband asked who gave me the garland.
a1 I answered that he had.
(c2 He did not accept that.)
r2 I swore that it was true.

vi.86g   qAqa
q1   Glaucus asked if he should steal the money with an oath.
A1   Oracle: Go ahead for short-run profit, but payment will come.
q2   Glaucus asked the god to forgive him for the question.
a2   The oracle said that making trial of the god and doing the deed were equal.

ix.111   CRCR
C1   Xerxes: Give up your wife and take my daughter.
R1   Masistes: I am honored but will do neither.
C2   Xerxes: Now you shall have neither, so you will learn to accept favors.
R2   Masistes: You have not destroyed me yet.

First response incomplete or inadequate (11)

iii.134; iv.145   (see p. 28)

i.119.5–7   qaqa
q1   Astyages asked if he was pleased with his dinner.
a1   Harpagus said he was very pleased.
q2   Astyages asked if he recognized what animal he had eaten.
a2   Harpagus said yes and that everything the king did pleased him.

iii.38.3–4   qaqa   (Here the two-stage tetrad achieves difference and development between the two pairs by the use of two contrasted respondents. It seems as if the two-stage pattern was being parodied, since it is not the responses that differ but the respondents, whose answers are in substance the same. The progression supposedly inherent in the pattern is here not a matter of time but of space.)
q1   Darius asked for how much money the Greeks would eat their dead fathers.
a1   The Greeks said for no amount.
q2   Darius asked for how much the Callatians would burn their dead fathers.
a2   The Callatians cried out against such impieties.

iii.74–75   crcr
c1   The magi appealed to him to keep silent about the deceit.
r1   Prexaspes agreed to do this.
c2   The magi appealed to him to announce that Smerdis was king.
r2   Prexaspes said he was ready.

iii.85   CRC(r)
C1   Darius: Fix it so I become king.
R1   Oibares: I have the means.
C2   Darius: Start fixing, since the contest is tomorrow.
(r2   Oibares acts.)

iii.128.4–5   C(r)C(r)
C1   Royal message: Darius forbids you to serve Oroetes.
(r1   Bodyguard throws down spears.)
C2   Royal message: Darius bids you kill Oroetes.
(r2   Bodyguard kills Oroetes.)
(In this case it is as if the volunteer Bagaeus, who arranged for the messages, took advantage of the two-stage pattern in order to effect Darius' purpose of disarming Oroetes without using force. The use of action-response in both pairs may indicate the pattern's preference for a nonverbal response when actions speak louder than words.)

iii.156   qa(q)A
q1   Babylonians asked who he was and what he wanted.
a1   Zopyrus said his name and that he was deserting to them.
(q2   He was brought to the assembly presumably for questioning.)
A2   Zopyrus: I come to benefit you and defeat Darius.

v.24   C(r)C(r)
C1   Darius: Come to me so that I may consult you.
(r1   Histiaeus came.)
C2   Darius: Come live in Susa and be my adviser.
(r2   Histiaeus went.)

v.82   qaqa
q1   Epidaurians asked about crop failure.
a1   Oracle said to make statues.
q2   Epidaurians asked if they were to be of stone or bronze.
a2   Oracle said they should be of olive wood.

vii.38–39   CrCR
C1   Pythius: I want to ask a favor.
r1   Darius said he would grant it.
C2   Pythius: Let one of my sons stay here.
R2   Darius: Shame on you; he will pay with his life.

Challenge-and-response dialogues involving command, reproach, or appeal tend to be more uniform in function than those made up of questions and answers. Commands and appeals, whether accepted and then augmented (ii.162; iii.74–75, 128; v.24; ix.11) or rejected and then successfully renewed (i.8; v.39), supply the people commanded or appealed to with an external stimulus to motivate the action that they consequently undertake. Even when the first command or appeal meets with neither acceptance nor outright rejection but an unsatisfactory response, the revised command or appeal serves to motivate action, but here it may be either consonant with the appeal (iii.46, 134) or in direct opposition to it (vi.129–130; ix.111). It is perhaps worth noting that the two-stage dialogues of command and appeal show more use of direct discourse than those involving questions and answers. This could be a reflection either of the more direct and immediate nature of commands and appeals or of the relative importance of the particular situations.

Variant and vestigial two-stage dialogues show some interesting features. (1) In both iv.133 and iv.136 the Scythians appeal to the Ionians to break the Danube bridge. The earlier appeal was anticipatory, since the sixty days of the agreement had not yet elapsed, but the Ionians agreed that they would. The later appeal, on the other hand, resulted in a debate among the Ionians with the resulting deceptive response advocated by Histiaeus, giving assurance to the Scythians that they were demolishing the bridge but preparing to fill the gap when Darius approached. The two appeals seem to be not so much stages but rather doublets that frame the episode in which Darius admits defeat and begins the withdrawal. It may be that the Ionian agreement to the first appeal is used to add to the hopelessness of Darius' situation and so justify his retreat, but in any case this is not a true two-stage tetrad. (2) Themistocles' lengthy appeal to the Greeks in viii.59–62 is interrupted twice by Adeimantus with reproaches that Themistocles answers: "Those who jump the gun in the games are penalized." "And those who are left behind are not crowned" (viii.59). And in viii.61: Adeimantus urged that cityless men be quiet and not allowed to vote; Themistocles made it clear that with 200 ships Athens was more of a city than Corinth. Not only are these two exchanges of taunts a kind of two-stage dialogue, but the second taunt by its rejection of the first part of Themistocles' appeal (60) allows the second part (62) to take on the threatening character so characteristic of second-stage challenges. Thus there is a kind of intertwining of two two-stage dialogues.

Chiastic Pairs (9)

ii.160; viii.88 (see p. 30)

i.37–40 CCRR
C1 Atys: How can I face my bride and others? Let me join the hunt.
C2 Croesus: I am only trying to protect you from the dream I had of your death.
R1 Atys: But a boar wields no iron weapon.
R2 Croesus: You win; you may go.

i.129   qqaa
q1   Harpagus asked how slavery was in contrast to kingship.
q2   Astyages asked if he was responsible for Cyrus' successful coup.
a1   Harpagus said he was.
a2   Astyages said that then he was the most stupid and unjust of men.

i.152–153   cq(a)R
c1   Herald said that Cyrus was to harm no Greek city; Sparta would not permit it.
q2   Cyrus asked who the Spartans were and how many.
(a1   Certain Greeks present told him.)
R2   Cyrus: I do not fear men who set aside a place to cheat each other.

vi.50   cqaR
c1   Crius said he (Cleomenes) could not take hostages without the other king.
q2   Cleomenes asked him what his name was.
a1   Crius said what it was.
R2   Cleomenes: Bronze your horns, Ram, trouble's coming.

viii.140–144   CCRR
C1   Alexander (to Athenians): Come over to the Persians.
C2   Spartans: Do not betray Greece.
R1   Athenians (to Alexander): We shall never obey barbarians.
R2   Athenians (to Spartans): We shall never betray Greece.
     (Not only is this the most Thucydidean of Herodotean dialogues, but also, and perhaps therefore, it fits least neatly into the chiastic-tetrad pattern in which the first Athenian response should be to the second [Spartan] challenge. But for the sake of both drama and ideology the patriotic manifesto must come last.)

ix.90–91   cQAR
c1   Hegesistratus appealed for help.
Q2   Leotychidas: What is your name?
A1   Hegesistratus: It is Hegesistratus.
R2   Leotychidas: I accept the omen.

ix.109   cQar
c1   Xerxes ordered Artaynte to ask for anything.
Q2   Artaynte: Will you really give me anything I ask?
a1   Xerxes swore an oath.
r2   Artaynte asked for the cloak.

Other Tetrads (9)

All other tetrads are made up of two more or less loosely connected pairs. One that has three speakers with its third speech looking both backward and forward is most like a Homeric tetrad in *Iliad* 6.324:

viii.100–102   CrQA
C1   Mardonius: Either fight on land or let me do it.
r1   Xerxes said he would take counsel and then decide.
Q2   Xerxes: This is what Mardonius advises; what do you say?
A2   Artemisia: Let him do it; the glory will be yours, and a failure his.

In other examples the first pair merely provides the situation to which the second pair reacts.

i.11   C(r)QA
C1   Queen: Choose to kill or be killed.
(r1   Gyges begged her not to force the choice but chose to kill.)
Q2   Gyges: Since you force me to kill, how do we do it?
A2   Queen: In the same fashion that you spied on me.

i.27   qACR
q1   Croesus asked if there was news.
A1   Sage: The islanders are buying horses to invade Lydia.
C2   Croesus: Would that they might attack.
R2   Sage: They pray similarly about you taking to the sea.

iv.131–132   qacR
q1   Persians asked the meaning of the gifts.
a1   Messenger said he had no orders about that.
c2   Darius' opinion was that they were symbolic of earth and water.
R2   Gobryas: No, they are asserting their invincibility in all elements.
     (The second pair here are basically opposite reactions not so much to the
        first pair as to the gifts themselves.)

iv.134   q(a)CR
q1   Darius asked what the commotion was among the Scythians.
(a1   He was told that they were chasing a hare.)
C2   Darius: If that is all they care about us, we must plan retreat.
R2   Gobryas: Let us leave campfires burning and steal away by night.

vii.8–11   CRCR
C1   Xerxes: I plan an expedition to Greece.
R1   Mardonius: A very good thing for the following reasons.
C2   Artabanus: Not a very good thing to do for these reasons.
R2   Xerxes: You are a coward; I shall go ahead and subdue Greece.
     (Like *Iliad* 6.324 and viii.100–102 above, this tetrad involves three speak-
        ers and a third speech that looks both ways, but it is similar in another
        way to iv.131–132 because there are two opposing reactions. Here
        there is a decision between the two, soon to be rescinded, whereas
        there the decision awaits on subsequent developments.)

vii.140–141   CrQA
C1   Oracle: Flee to the ends of the earth. All is ruin.

r1 Timon advised the Athenians to address the oracle as suppliants.
Q2 Athenians: We shall not go till you give us better news.
A2 Oracle: O holy Salamis, etc.

vii.148 qAcr
q1 Argives ask oracle what to do.
A1 Oracle: Guard your head, and the head will save the body.
c2 Greek messengers came asking Argives to join against Persia.
r2 Argives agreed but made impossible conditions.

ix.45–46 CrCR
C1 Alexander: Mardonius will attack. Tell Pausanias.
r1 Athenian generals reported the message.
C2 Pausanias: In the attack it will be better for Athenians to face Persians.
R2 Athenians: We think so too.

As far as function in the narrative goes, these other tetrads are used both to motivate someone to act and to explain and justify actions or characterize individuals or relationships. The function, as with other dialogues, often depends on the nature of the final speech: announcements or predictions and advice, commands, and appeals tend to motivate, whereas acceptances, rejections, warnings, and expressions of intent tend to explain. Mostly motivating as well as characterizing persons and clarifying issues are i.11; iv.134; vii.8–11; and viii.100–102. More explanatory of the general situation are i.27; iv.131–132; vii.140–141, 148; ix.45–46. In this connection it is worth noting that Herodotus did not, when faced with the two oracles to Athens (vii.140–141), present them in a two-stage tetrad with the first pair made up of an Athenian question answered by an unsatisfactory oracle and the second pair (as it is now) presenting a renewal of the request and a better result. It may be that the tradition of Timon's role was too lively to be passed over, but the tetrad-pattern seems to have prevailed so that there is no initial questioning of the oracle at all. Or was that "historical"?

PENTADS

Of the 16 independent pentads 11 combine a pair with a triad, 9 in that order and 2 with the triad preceding the pair. Not only is the triad-pair order very much in the minority, but also the 2 examples are odd in other respects as well. But the 9 pair-triad examples show a surprising regularity: a typical question-and-answer or challenge-and-response pair is followed by a typical thesis-antithesis-synthesis triad in which thesis and antithesis may be either question and answer or challenge and response.

Pair-Triad (or Tetrad-Single)

i.90, 111–112; v.49–50; ix.16 (see pp. 31–32)

ii.115   qa/qaS

Pair: Proteus asked who he was and whence he was sailing.
Paris said who he was and whence he was sailing.
Triad: Proteus asked whence he had taken Helen.
Paris lied but the servants told.
Proteus: I do not kill foreigners or you would pay; go, but leave her.

The answer in the triad is not fully indirect speech, but its dual nature and the pattern-function that it fulfills justify its inclusion in this dialogue. This pentad provides a demonstration of the way in which a two-stage tetrad might be augmented: the first pair is in itself an epic pattern useful in a variety of situations, while the second pair is concerned with Helen and the specific situation and at the same time motivates the fifth speech, much in the same way that other two-stage tetrads motivate action. The order of the speakers is *ab aba*, so that the one who asks the questions is the one who gives an order (or makes a promise or draws a conclusion) on the basis of information provided in the answers of his opposite number. The use of direct quotation for Proteus' final speech suggests not only that this was the only one of the dialogue that had real substance over and above the typical catechism but also that it was felt that the retention of Helen and dismissal of Paris needed full explanation.

v.51   cr/crS

Pair: Aristagoras urged that Cleomenes send away the child and listen to him.
Cleomenes urged him to say what he wished and not mind the child.
Triad: Aristagoras promised Cleomenes money if he would cooperate.
Cleomenes kept refusing.
Gorgo: Father, the foreigner will corrupt you if you do not go away.

Several of these speeches are as much narrative reporting as they are indirect discourse; moreover, the attempt at bribery was not single but a matter of escalation. On these grounds there might be question as to whether this is a true five-speech dialogue. The chief reason for thus classifying it is the similarity between this final direct speech and those in other pentads of this pair-triad form; these speeches provide a solution of a problem that has been given definition in the preceding pairs; the solution may be a compromise, a cutting of the Gordian knot, or a smart idea, but the general effect is that of a punchline. What is most entertaining here is the apparent foresight shown by Aristagoras in asking that the child be sent away. This seems to be an example of backcasting in which the narrator's knowledge of what is coming informs the preceding narrative. It was not enough to note that Aristagoras came in to find the girl with Cleomenes; for anyone who knew that it was she who would thwart the petitioner, it seemed only right that he should make an effort to have her removed.

      v.105   q(a)/CrS
Pair: Darius asked who the Athenians were.
      (He was told.)
Triad: Darius: Zeus, grant that I may punish Athens.
      Darius ordered his servant to repeat at dinner:
      "Master, remember the Athenians."

It is obvious that here only Darius speaks, whether directly or indirectly, since even the answer to his question is not given in words. Still, the effect of the whole is comparable to that of a pentad, since the result of asking a question and learning the answer is three speeches, of which the first is certainly a challenge and the third is a kind of solution combined with punchline. Whether this anecdote about Darius' reaction to the news of Sardis' burning has been attracted into the pentad form for the sake of this punchline is a possible question.

      vi.52   qa/qas
Pair: Spartans asked queen which child was the elder.
      Queen said she did not know.
Triad: Spartans asked Delphi what to do.
      Delphi said to make both kings but honor elder more.
      Panites advised them to observe mother's order of tending children.

It is worth noting that the two questions are not the same, as they often are in successive pairs when the two respondents are different. The presumption here is that the form of the second question has been influenced by the kind of answer that was both oracular in its ambiguity and in need of the solution to be provided in a typical synthesized reaction. Why the final speech is not dignified by direct reporting is difficult to determine, but the fact that the whole story is already in indirect discourse may help to explain.

viii.26 qa/qaS
Pair: Persians asked deserters what the Greeks were doing.
Deserters said they were holding the Olympic games.
Triad: Persians asked what was the prize for which they contested.
Deserters said it was an olive crown.
Tritantaechmes: What men we face, who contest not for money but for excellence!

The final speech is not in any strict sense a solution, but as a punchline it does justify and give point to the exchange leading up to it. The two questions follow the two-stage pattern of step-by-step inquiry.

Triad-Pair

The first example of a triad-pair pentad is one that includes a parenthetic triad reminiscent of a Homeric pentad, that in *Iliad* 1 (173 ff.) where after two tetrads (Achilles-Calchas-Achilles-Calchas, Agamemnon-Achilles-Agamemnon-Achilles) the pentad is made up as follows: challenge by Agamemnon that he will take Briseis brings quarrel to a head; response by Achilles has to be engineered by Athena, so the parenthetic triad of Achilles-Athena-Achilles is inserted after the challenge; synthesis by Nestor attempting reconciliation completes the triad of the pentad; the renewed challenge and response of the following pair (Agamemnon-Achilles) is in consequence somewhat more subdued, but that the dialogue should end in continued hostility is essential for the plot of the wrath-story. Thus there is good reason why the triad with its attempted reconciliation must not come at the end.

The Herodotean parallel (iii.34–35) is interrupted in mid-speech by a historical parenthesis that explains a reference in the speech, thus providing a splendid example of the way in which Herodotus includes material only as and when it becomes necessary.

iii.34–35 QAS(qaS)S/QA
Triad: Cambyses: What do the Persians think and say of me?
Prexaspes: They praise you except for your excessive love of wine.
Cambyses: Then their former words were not true. (*Parenthetic Triad.*)
Now if I can shoot your boy in the heart, they are proved wrong.

The shot

Pair: Cambyses: So it is clear that I am not crazed by drink. Have you ever seen such a good shot?
Prexaspes: Not even the god could shoot so well.

The parenthetic triad is made up of indirect question and answer with directly quoted "synthesis" that is actually antithetic to the answer: Cambyses had asked how he was in relation to his father, and his counselors had answered that he was better, but Croesus said, "Not the equal, since you have not a son such as he had." The triad is not necessary to the point of the pentad anecdote except in explaining the reference to the previous conversation, but Herodotus may have been struck by the contrast between the cleverness of Croesus' answer and Prexaspes' inept truthfulness. The triad-pair order here may not be an intentional reflection of Cambyses' unbalanced state, but in view of the pentad pattern's consistency elsewhere in the *Histories*, this reversal of pair and triad contributes to the anecdote's general feeling of perversity. Moreover, although Cambyses may give expression to his madness in a pseudo-rational synthesis, the only safe conclusion to the episode for his victim is a careful acquiescence.

The only other five-speech dialogue with triad-pair order is questionable both as a whole and in its parts:

iv.114–115 CR(s)/C(r)

Triad: Scythians: Let us take you home and you can be our wives.
Amazons: Better to claim your property and live apart.
(The Scythians agreed.)
Pair: Amazons: Better still, let us go completely out of this land.
(The Scythians agreed.)

Two things differentiate this dialogue from pattern pentads: the "silent" agreement of the Scythians in both triadic synthesis and paired response; and the triad-pair order. Both contribute materially to the overall impression of the anecdote: that strong-minded Amazons were more than a match for the Scythian men.

Single-Tetrad

The five pentads that combine a single speech with a tetrad all have the same form: the first speech is in the nature of an announcement

or provides some information which evokes the following questions
and answers or challenges and responses.

i.86   I(nformation)/qAqa
Single: Croesus: Solon (3 times).
Tetrad: Interpreters asked whom he invoked.
        Croesus: One whom I would have all tyrants heed.
        Interpreters asked what he meant.
        Croesus said he was an Athenian who had foreseen this end.

This tetrad is of the two-stage sort, with the obscurity of the first
answer evoking the second question. The final speech ties back to the
single, so that the function of the whole dialogue appears to be the
explanation as well as the motivation for behavior on Cyrus' part that
is both unexpected and out of character.

iii.140   i/QaCR
Single: Syloson said he was a benefactor of the King.
Tetrad: Darius: Who is he and what does he want?
        Syloson said he was the donor of the cloak.
        Darius: I will make you rich so you will never regret that deed.
        Syloson: No riches, but restore to me my fatherland without blood-
        shed or slavery.

Into this dialogue have been inserted two intermediaries, presumably
to adapt a generalized pattern to the situation of a foreign court: first,
Syloson's announcement has to be carried to Darius by the gate-
keeper; and second, after Darius has asked him about Syloson and he
has brought Syloson in, it is interpreters who repeat (indirectly)
Darius' question. Once the scene is made plausible by this acknowl-
edgment of the language difficulty, however, the interpreters are forgotten, and the dialogue continues in an ordinary fashion.* The tetrad
itself, as so often, is composed of a question-and-answer pair establishing identity and then a challenge-and-response pair incorporating
a proposal that leads through its acceptance, reformation, or rejection
to some subsequent action, which the dialogue both motivates and
explains.

---

*The parallel that most immediately comes to mind is the situation in *Odyssey* 11,
where at first the dead drink of the blood before they can speak, but once the method
of communication is established the mechanics may be forgotten. This is surely an
oral-narrative technique: the storyteller may often be forced, in order to forestall questions, to explain how a particular unusual event came about, but both he and his
audience, once they have taken that fence, feel themselves reestablished on firm
ground with no further need to cumber the narrative with repeated explanations.

v.73   (i)/q(a)cr

Single: Athenian messengers said what they had been ordered (to get Persian alliance).

Tetrad: Artaphernes asked who and whence they were.
(He learned from the messengers.)
Artaphernes promised alliance if they gave earth and water.
They agreed to give.

Again the question-and-answer pair establishing identity is followed by a challenge-and-response pair incorporating a proposal that is accepted. Herodotus notes that the messengers were blamed at home for the acceptance, but turning as he does to another part of the present digression he never follows up this exchange nor uses it to explain events that might well have resulted from Athenian acceptance of Persian overlordship: Artaphernes' order to them to take Hippias back and the resultant open hostility as of revolting subjects (v.96.2); Darius' particular desire to punish the Athenians after the burning of Sardis as perhaps more appropriate if they have sworn allegiance (v.105). The dialogue is thus used more to finish off one part of this long digression rather than to explain or motivate anything.

vii.14–18 I/CRCR

Single: Dream: Know well, if you do not make this expedition, you will soon lose your power.

Tetrad: Xerxes: See if the same dream comes to you.
Artabanus: Dreams are not so directed, but I will try it.
Dream: Do not try to help Xerxes evade his fate.
Artabanus (to Xerxes): I withdraw opposition, so go ahead.

Oddly enough, the first pair of the tetrad is concerned with identification, even though there is no question except whether the dream will be able to distinguish between Xerxes and Artabanus. The first pair also sets the scene for the second pair, which explains how Xerxes came to be encouraged to make the expedition even by the uncle who had originally opposed it. The whole exchange has the effect of relieving Xerxes of enough of the responsibility for the expedition so that his life is not implicated in its failure.

viii.137   i/crCR

Single: Queen told her husband about the size of Perdiccas' loaf.

Tetrad: King told the boys to leave.
They said they should be paid.

King (pointing to sun on floor): This is your wage.
Perdiccas (cutting it out): We accept.

Herodotus is here surely repeating a traditional tale that attributed the origin of the Macedonian royal power to the cleverness and special genius of a youngest son. The folktale's use of a pentad combining a single speech and a tetrad demonstrates the basic nature of the form and suggests that other dialogue patterns as well were grounded in traditional tales where they served the same explanatory and motivating function that they have in the *Histories*.

HEXADS

Hexad Pattern One: Three Pairs (6)

Three-Stage Pairs

v.13 (see p. 33)

iii.71–73   CRCRCR
Pair: Since so many know, we should act promptly.
        Otanes: No, better go slow; we need more men to act.
Pair: Darius: Beware of treachery; I myself will betray if we do not act immediately.
        Otanes: Since you force us to act, how are we to do it? (Cf. i.11.)
Pair: Darius: We can easily deceive the guards or fight our way in.
        Gobryas: We must do it; let us follow Darius' advice.

The three-stage pairs here are clear: Darius' outline of the situation constitutes the first challenge; Otanes' rejection of that evokes Darius' second challenge, to which Otanes' response is both acceptance and a question; that question is answered with a new challenge, to which Gobryas replies with a motivating speech that comes back around to Darius' original challenge. But at the same time the last three speeches also conform to a familiar triadic pattern, since the question in Otanes' second speech is answered by Darius in such a way that Gobryas brings the conspirators all together in his synthesizing reaction. It may be that the whole hexad should be viewed not only as three pairs but also as two triads that mirror each other: the second is the normal question-answer-synthesis; the first, as mirror-image, would be synthesis-response-challenge, with Darius announcing at the beginning of the hexad what Gobryas recommends at the end.

The second triad builds on the first, with the second speaker becoming the first as the roles reverse and as the previous petitioner becomes the petitioned; but at the same time the alternation between the two speakers is preserved. Although symmetry might then require that the third speech of the second triad be Otanes, the original objector and the subsequent petitioner, both verisimilitude and the need for at least one other conspirator's participation make desirable the introduction of Gobryas. Not only do Otanes' original reluctance and later abdication from the contest make an enthusiastic endorsement unlikely, but also Gobryas' later prominence with Darius in the slaughter of the Magi makes him an appropriate supporter. The very disruption of the pattern (from expected *ababab* to *ababac*) gives an impression of outside support and so a general willingness on the part of the conspirators to implement Darius' original proposal. The introduction of a third speaker is by itself sufficiently unusual to signal something special, since Herodotus, like contemporary tragedians, presents three-way conversations only rarely.

The two other three-stage pairs are comparatively simple and uncomplicated.

     i.120   qaQACR

Pair: Astyages asked in what way they judged his dream.
       The seers said it was necessary for the boy to rule if he lived.
Pair: Astyages: He lives and acted as king among boys. What do you think?
       Seers: He has fulfilled the dream if this happened without your contrivance.
Pair: Astyages: I agree but want your advice as to what will be best now.
       Seers: Rest assured that there is no danger; send the boy to his parents.

Three pairs connected in linear fashion build up to a conclusion that motivates the subsequent action, thus tying together the dream and its attempted evasion, to which the first pair harks back, and what amounts to a rejection of the dream with advice that will prepare the way for its fulfillment. The pairs of speeches in this hexad function in much the same way as the individual speeches in the thesis-antithesis-synthesized-reaction triad: the present interpretation answers and is opposed to the past interpretation, so that out of the contradiction comes a new beginning. The first pair is in indirect discourse because it merely resumes and repeats an earlier exchange. The second pair would have finished off a two-stage tetrad designed to explain Astyages' willingness to let Cyrus live, but because his sending of the boy to Persia also seemed to require motivation, a third pair was added. Some awkwardness resulted, since the appeal for advice was largely a repetition of the previous question.

iii.68–69   qaCRCr
Pair: Otanes asked his daughter with whom she slept, Smerdis or another.
Phaedime said she did not know, and had never seen Smerdis, son of Cyrus.
Pair: Otanes: If you do not know, ask Atossa.
Phaedime: I cannot; we are all separated.
Pair: Otanes: You must look to see if the man you sleep with has ears.
Phaedime replied that it was risky but she would do it.

The indirect reporting of the first pair, like that of the hexad above (i.120), puts the basic but ineffectual first question and answer in proper proportion. The indirect reporting of Phaedime's final response is, however, more difficult to explain. That it indicates the comparative unimportance of that response is clear, but only one explanation of that unimportance comes immediately to mind: that, as so often with dialogues, this one motivates action, and Otanes' challenge or command in and of itself fulfills that function without the necessity of her reply. Thus the present form of the dialogue may represent an uneasy compromise between the regular three-pair hexad and a pentad made up of a pair (qa) and a triad (CRS) with its last speech serving as a synthesizing reaction to the thesis and antithesis of challenge and response. The almost parenthetical second pair here may well be the kind of thing that a storyteller is obliged to insert in response to questions from an alert audience, or it may simply be in the interests of verisimilitude, like Cambyses' question to the messenger in the dialogue with Prexaspes (iii.62; see below under Heptads). There too the same kind of three-stage pair is used to answer the question of how an interested party learned who the usurper was.

Tetrad and Pair

vii.101–104   QQaA/CR
Tetrad: Xerxes: Will the Greeks resist?
Demaratus: Do you want the truth?
Xerxes said yes and not to fear.
Demaratus: Yes, they will, no matter what the odds.

Pair: Xerxes: Would you take on ten or twenty men? Could any army without a single master stand up to mine?
   Demaratus: Perhaps not, but I would try one of those who wish to take on three Greeks. Law is our single master.

The tetrad here is chiastic in arrangement, being made up of one question-and-answer pair in the middle and one at the extremes. The resulting separation of the two parts of the substantive pair by what amounts to a validating pair serves both to underline and to guarantee Demaratus' answer. In the concluding pair Xerxes' incredulity serves the double purpose of showing his culpable heedlessness of warning and of evoking Demaratus' modest assertions of personal prowess and national strength. The inner dynamics of this hexad are thus complex in a way that the previous examples of pairs related in linear fashion are not; only with the tetrad (extreme question-and-answer pair reinforced or fortified by the median question-and-answer pair) as background does the concluding pair of challenge and response make sense, not because it continues the step-by-step progress of the linear pairs but because it raises discussion from the particular to a universal plane in order to make an ideological point. This triple exchange motivates nothing, but it does both explain why the Persian multitude will not sweep all before it and show how Xerxes' arrogance blinded him to strengths and values different from his own. Presenting as it does some of the basic ideological and historical forces that Herodotus found operating in the Greek-Persian conflict, this hexad is most comparable to the question-and-answer pairs that make explicit Herodotus' principles of historical interpretation: i.30–32, the need to judge by the end; vii.209, the superiority of mind over matter, spirit over force, law over the lash.

   The next hexad, although it is also made up of tetrad and pair, serves as a transition to the two-triad hexad below, since its last three speeches might be regarded as making up a regular thesis-antithesis-synthesis triad:

   vii.234–237 QAQA/CR
Tetrad: Xerxes: You were right. But how many more are there like these?
   Demaratus: 8,000 Spartiates, and other brave Lacedaemonians.
   Xerxes: How can they most easily be defeated?
   Demaratus: By occupying Cythera and so dividing them from the rest of Greece.

Pair: Achaemenes: Do not heed one who envies your success; dividing
          the fleet is a mistake.
          Xerxes: Demaratus means well, but you are right.

In the tetrad Xerxes' question about how to defeat the Spartans takes
on a special irony in the context of their comparatively tiny numbers;
it is not news of overwhelming Spartan strength that motivates his
plea for advice, which would be the situation in two question-and-
answer pairs related in linear fashion. It is rather the absurdity of the
master of millions worrying first about the possible number of the
enemy and then of asking how to cope with what turns out to be
barely a fraction of his forces; only the interlocking of these two pairs
conveys the irony. The concluding pair, which introduces a new
speaker, is clearly motivated by the last speech of the tetrad, since
Achaemenes opposes Demaratus' advice. But the very opposition
between Demaratus and Achaemenes brings their two speeches together as thesis and antithesis of a triad to which Xerxes' final speech
gives the synthesis. And that speech not only arbitrates between the
two advisers but also rounds out the whole hexad as it harks back to
Xerxes' first speech: there he acknowledged how right Demaratus
had been in his earlier advice; now his judgment that Demaratus was
wrong demonstrates once again his inability to learn without further
suffering. The function of the dialogue is therefore explanatory.

Hexad Pattern Two: Two Triads (1)

The two-stage triads that make up the following hexad are neither
fully articulate nor much more than doublets for cumulative effect,
but they do show the way in which triads can be used in the same
step-by-step build-up as that of two-stage pairs in tetrads:

          iii.27–28   qas/(q)as
Triad: Cambyses asked why they were celebrating now.
          The governors said that a god had appeared to them.
          Cambyses said they lied.
Triad: (Cambyses summoned the priests.)
          The priests said the same.
          Cambyses said no god could come without his knowledge.

The first triad establishes Cambyses' state of mind; the accumulated
effect of the second triad moves him to action and so motivates the
order that the Apis be brought to him.

Hexad Pattern Three: Single Plus Pentad (Pair-Triad)

vii.27–29 i//qA/qAS

Single: Pythius announced that he wished to furnish money for the expedition.

Pair: Xerxes asked who Pythius was and how much money he had.

Persians: He is the son of so-and-so and has the most money of any we know.

Triad: Xerxes asked Pythius how much money he had.

Pythius: 2,000 talents of silver and almost 4 million gold darics, all for you.

Xerxes: Thank you, but let me rather round out the sum for you.

The pentad is evoked by the announcement much in the same way that independent pentads are evoked by a particular action, as for example Mitradates' return home with the baby Cyrus (i.111) or Paris' arrival at Proteus' court (ii.115). But the very fact that it is a speech which gives rise to the pentad influences both form and content so that first and last speeches mirror each other in their grandiose offers. These are neatly contrasted, the one expressed indirectly and evoking a question-and-answer pair, the other evoked by a question-and-answer pair and expressed directly and with lordly condescension. At the same time the two intervening pairs are very much like a two-stage tetrad which makes the transition from first speech to last. What could have been a four-speech dialogue made up of a single announcement and simple question-answer-reaction triad has been inflated by letting two question-and-answer pairs do the work of one.

vii.157–162 I//CR/CRS

Single: Greeks: The Persian is coming to enslave Greece; it is to your interest to help.

Pair: Gelon: Though you did not help me, I will help you, but I must be supreme commander.

Spartan: No! Sparta commands. Either follow or stay home.

Triad: Gelon: I am more generous than you and will share the command with you—fleet or army.

Athenian: Never fleet! If Sparta does not command that, we do.

Gelon: You have commanders in plenty, but what will they command?

One special feature of this dialogue is the division of the original speaker into two speakers who respond to the challenges; it is this split that results in the doubling of challenge and response. Besides being single and pentad, then, the hexad can be viewed as made up of contrasting initial and final speeches with intervening two-stage pairs. As in the previous dialogue, the original statement evokes one challenge-and response pair, and the final statement is provoked by a second challenge-and-response pair. Here too the challenges (or questions) have the same thrust and content while the responders differ in person but only partly in response. And just as Xerxes' final speech amounted to a refusal of Pythius' initial offer, so here Gelon's final statement is a denial of the Greeks' original appeal; in both cases the final speech is explained and illuminated by the intervening pairs.

HEPTADS

i.88–89   Qa/QAS//qA   Pentad//pair
Pentad of Pair and Triad
Pair: Croesus: Should I say what I think?
        Cyrus told him to go ahead without fear.
Triad: Croesus: What are those men of yours doing?
        Cyrus: They are looting your city.
        Croesus: Not my city but yours.

Pair
Cyrus asked what Croesus would advise him to do about it.
Croesus: Arrange to have everything turned in so that tithe can be taken out.

This pentad closely resembles independent pentads like i.90, 111–112; ii.115; viii.26; ix.16, and dependent pentads like vii.27–29, 46–52, where one pair of question and answer or challenge and response leads to a second pair, which is capped by a fifth speech in which the original questioner or challenger justifies and implements his original appeal. When such a pentad is followed by a pair, as here, the fifth speech is not an end in itself but a means to effect a reversal of roles so that the person previously appealed to now makes the appeal. That the heptad is in another way more than the sum of its parts is apparent from the symmetry of the two pairs framing a central triad and their mirror-reversal: in the first pair Croesus questions directly and Cyrus answers indirectly; in the second Cyrus questions indirectly and Croesus answers directly. Not only are the indirectly reported speeches rendered comparatively unimportant, but also the role of Cyrus is played down thereby and Croesus' role is emphasized. This emphasis is made more dramatic by the contrast between the apparent diffidence of Croesus' first question and the confidence displayed in his answer to Cyrus' request for advice.

      i.158–159   qaQa/QAS   Tetrad/triad

Tetrad: Cumaeans asked oracle about giving up suppliant.
      Oracle said to go ahead.
      Aristodicus: What shall we do about the suppliant?
      Oracle gave the same answer.
Triad: Oracle: Are you tearing away my suppliants?
      Aristodicus: Do you protect yours and advise us to give up ours?
      Oracle: I so advised that you might sooner learn not to ask about giving up suppliants.

This dialogue differs from the previous one in two interrelated ways: the number of speakers is three instead of two; and there is an interval of reaction or action both between the two pairs of the tetrad and between tetrad and triad. It is only the interval of reaction and the change in questioner that allows the second question and answer to be the same as the first, but the repetition with a new questioner (especially one whose directly quoted question points him up as the real interlocutor in the confrontation to come) shows the build-up of question-and-answer pair on question-and-answer pair characteristic of other tetrads so that the interval of reaction may be overlooked.* Similarly, it is only by inserting Aristodicus' attack on the birds nesting around the temple between tetrad and triad that a typical punch-line triad can be used here. Is there then some suggestion that dialogue patterns exert some kind of influence on the narrative to pull it into a particular shape? Thus in order that the oracle's final riposte may both cap a question-and-answer exchange and provide the true divine reaction to the Cumaeans' first question, it was necessary first to individualize that question in a second question-and-answer pair and then allow that individual so to provoke the oracle that roles were switched and the oracle became questioner. If someone objects and asks why we should not believe that it happened just as Herodotus has told it (with a priest speaking for Apollo), the only answer at present must be the neatness with which the oracle's justification of impious and improper advice is motivated—a neatness more characteristic of fiction than of fact. It may be that later, when we have

---

*Compare two-stage pairs in which the questioner is the same and the question more of the same (i.116; iii.46, 51; v.39; vi.69) and cases in which the question is the same but the respondent is different (vi.52; vii.27–29).

explored other dialogues in which pattern elements seem to organize raw data, the weight of the evidence will help to support this suggestion.

iii.61–63   i/QAQAQA   Single/hexad
Single
Herald announced that Smerdis was now king.
Hexad (three pairs)
Pair: Cambyses: Is it thus that you carry out my orders?
        Prexaspes: This is not true, for I myself buried Smerdis. Ask from whom the messenger received orders.
Pair: Prexaspes: Did Smerdis himself give you orders?
        Herald: I have never seen Smerdis; the magus instructed me.
Pair: Cambyses: Who then has usurped in Smerdis' name?
        Prexaspes: It must be the magus Patizeithes and his brother Smerdis.

There is a question whether this dialogue should include the indirect announcement of the herald as motivating factor or whether, as in other situations where the receipt of information leads to inquiry or discussion, it should be regarded as action outside the dialogue. The fact that the wording of the message is given, even though indirectly ("in the future obedience is to be given to Smerdis son of Cyrus rather than to Cambyses"), distinguishes this arrival of news from that in cases where there is only narrative, e.g., i.155.2, "Cyrus having learned this said to Croesus . . ."; i.212.1, "Tomyris, having heard what had happened to the army, said . . ." Furthermore, the reappearance of the herald in the second question-and-answer pair ties in his original announcement more closely so that the order of speakers is *a*/BC/CA/BC. The herald's second announcement serves also as a pivot, being evoked by the previous speeches and evoking the following pair. This is one of the few dialogues in the *Histories* in which more than two persons converse, but here as in most of the others the exchanges are not three-way but between only two persons at a time. The form of the hexad is influenced by the number of speakers (compare iii.71–73 and vii.234–237), but as in the case of several two-stage pairs, what was needed here was a realistic representation of the way in which someone came to know something that was to affect his actions. In this case a two-stage question-and-answer dialogue made up of the first and third pairs above was not sufficient, since no Persian king mad enough to order his brother's death was likely to accept the unsupported assertion of his agent. Therefore the second pair had to be inserted, and it is typical of Herodotus' narrative habits that even this question is motivated by the suggestion of Prexaspes, who could be assumed to be self-motivated because he had a personal stake in Cambyses' learning the truth. Cambyses' apparent willingness to accept Prexaspes' word and Smerdis' death on the basis of the hearld's not very complete evidence is partly dramatic necessity and partly the effect of the question-and-answer pattern. It is presumably the pattern too that makes the otherwise suspicious Cambyses innocently ask who could have taken over Smerdis' name when Prexaspes was no better informed than he himself was.

OCTAD

The one octad (i.30–32) has already been outlined (pp. 26–27) in introducing those tetrads made up of two-stage pairs. As indicated there, this conversation between Croesus and Solon consists of four pairs of question and answer which have been welded first into two tetrads and then into the octad; the tetrads differ in that as one builds up the other builds down. The one speech that would have been almost an exact repetition of an earlier one is muted by the use of indirect discourse, and a masterly compromise has been achieved by naming two men as the second happiest; a third round of questions would have been excessive, but the oral narrative's affinity for the number three almost required that the happiest men be three in number.

ENNEAD

The nine speeches of v.18–20 are interspersed with action, but there are so many internal links and echoes that as an ennead whole the dialogue is more than the tetrad, pair, and triad that make it up. The first instance of interspersed action is between the two-stage pairs of the tetrad: the entrance of the women and their being seated opposite the Persians. This action is a necessary demonstration of the inadequacy and incompleteness of the first answer.

> v.18–20   CRc(r)/CR/C(r)C
> *Tetrad:*   Persians: Let us have your women.
>   Amyntas: It is not our custom but you are masters.
>   Persians said the distance was worse than no women.
>   (Amyntas ordered the women to sit beside the Persians.)

After the tetrad it is only through action (the Persians' improper advances to the women) that the adequacy of the second response to the Persian challenge can be demonstrated. At the same time this action demonstrates Amyntas' powerlessness and so motivates Alexander's intervention in a pivotal fifth speech in which the initiative shifts from Persians to Macedonians. Thus far, except for the intervening action, the tetrad-and-pair part of this ennead is most like the hexad of vii.234–237, where after the two-stage pairs a third speaker intervenes with advice which is accepted.

Pair: Alexander (to Amyntas): Let me manage; you go to bed.
          Amyntas (to Alexander): Be careful and be patient; I shall go.

Action again intervenes in the midst of the final triad and again involves movement on the part of the women, so that this last scene is symmetrical with the first. That symmetry is confirmed both by the way in which the Persian acquiescence here echoes Amyntas' double acquiescence in the first scene and by the way in which Alexander's final proposal comes around full circle to fulfill (with a vengeance!) the Persians' original challenge.

Triad: Alexander: Let the women bathe and come back.
          (Persians agreed.)
          Alexander, having replaced the women with disguised men: Here
          they are; have a good time.

After Alexander's final synthesis (of Persian license with Macedonian liberty) no more talk is necessary or desirable; the Persians, in a state of happy anticipation, have been set up for retribution, and one sentence is sufficient to finish the matter that has been so thoroughly motivated by the nine-speech dialogue. The whole story is a symphony of dialogue and action, but in this case the action seems to be subordinated to the dialogue in such a way as to produce the effect of a dramatic reading.

DECAD

vii.46–52 (see pp. 34–35)

DECAHEXAD

iii.21–23 (see pp. 34–36)

OTHER EXAMPLES

It seemed desirable to make my own collection of speeches without consulting any other listing or collection. Then, after classifying and drawing conclusions on the basis of my material, I could check with other studies and find that there were speeches I had missed. Such speeches would then serve as a test of my categories and interpretations, not having been taken into account in their formulation. So the figures given above and in Appendix III are of my collection and should be amended by the addition of the following examples culled from Paavo Hohti, *The Interrelation of Speech and Action in the Histories of Herodotus.**

Two indirect singles that fit neatly into the category of Class 2 explaining speeches: ii.172.4–5 in which Amasis uses the gold statue made from a slopbasin to justify his rise from lowly origins; ix.55.2 in which Amomphare-tus says that he is voting not to run from the Persians.
Two indirect pairs that fit into Pair Pattern 4 (motivation by question and answer): ix.5 Only in answer to Murychides' request that the Athenians medize does Lycidas urge acceptance, thus motivating his stoning.; ix.93.4 Only in answer to the Apollonians' question about their misfortunes do the oracles answer that Evenius must be compensated for his blindness, thus motivating the Apollonians' appeal to Evenius.
One mixed triad of the question-answer-synthesis (qaS) variety: ix.94 The Apollonians ask Evenius what he would consider adequate compensation; he answers, and the Apollonians make a formal speech of conferral. The whole is like so many triads in being more anecdotal, more characterizing, less necessary to the forward movement of the narrative than are most speeches and dialogues.

Thus the way in which these overlooked speeches† fit into the categories already established goes some way to confirming the validity of the classification. The change in overall numbers is not very important, but the new totals are as follows:

2 plus 85 indirect singles added to the 92 direct total 179 singles;
2 plus 51 indirect pairs added to 33 direct and 26 mixed total 112 pairs;
1 mixed triad added to 26 triads of all kinds total 27 triads.

*Hohti does not, by the way, include many of the speeches listed here, mostly of the following categories: direct single speeches which are quotations like i.199.3; ii.78; v.56.1; indirect singles of command, prayer, information, appeal, advice, or warning; pairs of qa or qA involving oracles; indirect pairs like i.122; iii.58.3; iv.84.1; vi.3; vii.151, 168.1, 218; ix.117; an indirect triad at ii.133 (involving an oracle); indirect tetrads at ii.162 and v.82; an indirect pentad (vi.52).

†Hohti counts as speeches two other examples which seem to me to fit neither his definitions nor mine: viii.83 a pre-battle exhortation that is described but not quoted indirectly; ix.41 a pair of opinions (*gnomai*) that are described but not expressly recorded as spoken.

Summary Survey
of Speeches' Formal Aspects

INTRODUCTIONS FOR DIRECTLY QUOTED SPEECHES

Table 1 summarizes the introductions of the 409 directly quoted speeches. As far as the totals are concerned, 47% of the 409 are introduced by the verb alone, 46% with a simple demonstrative pronoun, and 3.5% each with *toiade* and the others (*hōde* 6, *logon tonde* 3, *tosonde* 2, *hode chresmos* 1, *touto to epos* 1, *tade kai logou toioude echomena* 1). Except in the case of triads there appears to be a definite tendency to greater use of the verb alone as the dialogues become longer. It is likely that the anecdotal, dramatic nature of the triads militated against the use of demonstrative pronouns or other introductory words as belonging to narrative rather than drama. The same

Table 1

	Verb alone	Tade toiside	Toiade	Other
92 singles	32 (35%)	46 (50%)	8 (8.5%)	6 (6.5%)
92 in pairs	36 (39%)	48 (52%)	3 (3.5%)	5 (5.5%)
37 in triads	26 (70%)	11 (30%)		
79 in tetrads	29 (37%)	46 (58%)	2 (2.5%)	2 (2.5%)
36 in pentads	21 (58%)	15 (42%)		
33 in hexads	20 (61%)	11 (33%)	1 (3%)	1 (3%)
40 in longer ones	27 (67%)	12 (30%)	1 (3%)	—
Total	191	189	15	14

might be true of the longer dialogues, but there the avoidance of monotonous repetition is probably also an important factor. It may also be that it is the tetrads that are out of line, and the explanation of that would be their almost invariable make-up of pairs, so that they are most comparable to pairs in all forms of introduction.

With regard to the simple demonstrative pronoun, it should be noted that *toiside* is never used to introduce single speeches; this is because almost invariably it accompanies the verb "answer" (*ameibomai*). Concerning the use of *toiade*, it is possible that its function is to indicate that the point(s) made in the speech that follows are only a sample of possible arguments. And it may be that if the two uses of *tosonde* (i.199.3 and ix.111.5) are purposeful in implying that only so much was said and nothing more, the use of the qualitative demonstrative is also purposeful. In using *toiade* Herodotus may be avoiding commitment to particular statements in an attempt to forestall audience objection of one sort or another. For example, how could he know more than the general gist of confidential conversations between ruler and trusted aide (i.8.2, 108.3), between two brothers (iii.145.2), between son and mother (vi.68.1), between husband and wife (iii.134.2), between rulers making a secret deal (iv.80), and between others speaking in confidence (ii.173.2 and vi.86a, 86b)? Another objection which *toiade* might forestall could have been based on doubt that what the speaker had to say was sufficient to produce the result that followed (i.60.5; vii.158, 168.3; ix.17.4, 116.3). The only other use of *toiade* is to introduce the speech of the Ethiopian king (iii.21), which had to be relayed through the Fisheater interpreters.

Why more than half of the uses of *toiade* are to introduce single speeches is a puzzling question. It may be that a single speech represents less of a commitment on Herodotus' part to the detailed interpretation of a particular situation and so in some cases this tentativeness is emphasized by the vagueness of *toiade*. But the objection both here and to the suggestions above is that *toiade* is not used in all situations of these kinds.

LENGTHS OF SPEECHES

Table 2 summarizes speech lengths in the various dialogue patterns; figures are based on lines in the Oxford Classical Text. About a quarter of the speeches in pairs, triads, and tetrads, like the singles,

Table 2

	2 lines or less	10 lines or more	3–9 lines
Directly quoted			
92 singles	20 (22%)	18 (19%)	54 (59%)
92 in pairs	23 (25%)	17 (18%)	52 (57%)
37 in triads	10 (27%)	15 (41%)	12 (32%)
79 in tetrads	21 (27%)	20 (25%)	38 (48%)
36 in pentads	14 (39%)	7 (19%)	15 (42%)
33 in hexads	1 (3%)	14 (42%)	18 (55%)
40 in longer ones	12 (30%)	8 (20%)	20 (50%)

are very short (two lines or less); the use of such short speeches is less predictable in the longer dialogues. Long speeches are most prominent in triads and hexads but the numbers are probably not large enough to make the difference significant, since for triads the three speeches of the constitutional debate (iii.80–82) and the long speeches of Socles (v.92) and Leotychidas (vi.86) are enough to throw off the percentages. The same is true of hexads, where the Greek-Gelon debate (vii.157–162) has four long speeches and the two Xerxes-Demaratus dialogues (vii.101–104, 234–237) each have three. With these exceptions it is generally true that about half of all direct speeches range from three to nine lines in length. No particular conclusion can be drawn from these figures, but it is interesting to compare Herodotean totals with those for speeches in *Iliad* 1–12:

	Number of speeches	2 lines or less	10 lines or more	3–9 lines
Herodotus	409	101 (25%)	99 (24%)	209 (51%)
Iliad 1–12	312	19 (6%)	106 (34%)	187 (60%)

NUMERICAL NATURE OF SPEAKERS AND AUDIENCES

Table 3 shows the parts played by individuals and groups in Herodotean dialogue. Much the same proportions between individuals and groups hold for the various speakers of pentads, hexads, etc.; the range for individuals is from 67% to 89% with a corresponding high

Table 3

		Individual	Group
Singles:	speaker	85%	15%
	audience	40%	60%
Pairs:	first speaker	75%	25%
	second speaker	93%	7%
Triads:	first speaker	85%	15%
	second speaker	65%	35%
	third speaker	89%	11%
Tetrads:	first speaker	79%	21%
	second speaker	79%	21%
	third speaker	70%	30%
	fourth speaker	79%	21%

and low for groups of 33% and 11%. The groups involved in these dialogues are about equally divided between populations appealing, challenging, or reacting and generalized substitutes for a single individual where a particular individual either does not or should not stand out. Even so, the percentages contribute little or nothing to an understanding of Herodotus' use of dialogues. What does seem to be significant is the very large percentage of groups acting as audiences to single speeches and the very small percentage of groups providing the second speech of pairs. The explanation for both of these almost certainly lies in the chief functions of singles and pairs: just as the great majority of single speeches serve to motivate action, often the action of groups, and thus tend to have groups as their audience, so the majority of pairs' second speeches either provide amended motivation, rejection of action, explanation, or justification, all of which are more likely to be made by single individuals, or are motivating oracles that are regarded as the god speaking as a single individual.

The number of speakers in singles and pairs is obvious, but in dialogues made up of from three to sixteen speeches it is clear that the number of speakers might theoretically range from three to sixteen. In actual fact there is no dialogue in the *Histories* in which there are more than four participants. Of the 105 dialogues of three or more speeches, 70, or two-thirds, have only two speakers. The remaining third is divided as follows: 31 have three speakers; 4 have four. But among both three-speaker and four-speaker dialogues there are several cases where the third or fourth speaker is more illusive than real. Three of the four-speaker dialogues are in this category, with one of the speakers being a group from which one individual (or two) is (or are) separated out as the fourth (or third and fourth) speaker(s):

viii.137. Queen announces, king challenges, boys respond, king challenges, and Perdiccas (one of the boys) responds;

iv.131–132. Persians question, messenger answers, Darius concludes, Gobryas concludes (the two last are included among the Persians);

vii.157–162. Greek envoys appeal, Gelon challenges twice, and Syagrus and the Athenian envoy respond (the two last are included among the Greek envoys).

In all three cases the group speech could as well have been put in the mouth of the one or two individuals—that is, Perdiccas, Darius and Gobryas, and Syagrus and the Athenian envoy—except where there are two the difference between them is too important either to allow a duet or to give priority to one. The only four-speaker dialogue in which there are four entirely separate speakers is vi.52, but even here it is not a matter of a four-way conversation; rather it is three separate scenes brought together to make two pairs of questions (Spartans both times) and answers (queen and oracle), both of which are inadequate, capped by a solution (Panites).

Many of the three-speaker dialogues are similarly not real three-way conversations. The number three is illusive in one example because one of the two anonymous speakers is almost certainly part of the other: viii.88, someone announces; Xerxes asks; they answer; Xerxes comments. In another case of an individual breaking off from a group to become a third speaker, there is also some shifting of scenes and intervening action: i.158–159, Cumaeans ask; oracle responds; one of the Cumaeans (Aristagoras) puts the same question; the oracle responds; thereafter it is oracle, Aristagoras, oracle.

The various ways of handling three speakers can best be categorized by working up from triads to the longer and more complex dialogues. Triads with three speakers are of two kinds: (1) a questioner or challenger and two different or opposite respondents; (2) three different points of view. In the former case the dialogue is only superficially a three-way exchange, since the two respondents are related almost exclusively to the challenger or questioner:

iii.34.4–5. Cambyses asks; Persians answer one way; Croesus another.
iv.118–119. Scythians appeal; some chiefs accept; others reject.
viii.67–68. Mardonius asks; generals answer one way; Artemisia another.

(A reversal of this question-answer-answer triad is found in the question-question-answer of i.53: Croesus puts the question; the messengers ask it; the oracle answers.) Only in the second category is there a real three-way exchange:

iii.80–82. Otanes proposes; Megabyzus counterproposes; Darius answers both with a new proposal.

Halfway between the superficial and the real three-way exchange is a triad in which there are three points of view, but they are given expression in two two-way exchanges:

v.91–93 Spartans appeal; Socles rejects; Hippias answers rejection.

Among the three-speaker tetrads there are the following varieties: (1) a single speaker who provides the impetus or context for a two-speaker triad (*a/bcb*); (2) two two-speaker pairs (*abbc, abac, abca*), the first of which provides the context or impetus for the second; (3) interwoven two-speaker pairs (*abcc*). The single speaker in the first category is not actually necessary and could be replaced by narrative impetus or context for the two-way exchange, so that these dialogues are only nominally three-speaker dialogues:

i.152–153, Herald announces; Cyrus asks the Greeks who are present; they answer; Cyrus concludes (*a/bcb*).
ix.45–46. Alexander announces; Athenians report; Pausanias reacts; Athenians respond (*a/bcb*).

The second category ranges from (2a) two exchanges that are only superficially three-way and involve a change of scene, through (2b) three in which the two-way exchanges take place in a three-way situation, to (2c) two in which there is not only two-way exchange within the two pairs but also between them. This last group is very close to a true three-way exchange, although it is still firmly based on the two-way form:

(2a) vii.148. Argives ask; oracle answers; Greek envoys appeal; Argives reject (*abca*).
      viii.100–102. Mardonius challenges; Xerxes responds; Xerxes asks; Artemisia responds (*abbc*).

(2b)   iii.38. Darius asks; Greeks answer; Darius asks; Callatians answer
       (*abac*).
       iv.134. Darius asks; they answer; Darius asks; Gobryas answers (*abac*).
       vi.129–130. Cleisthenes challenges; Hippocleides responds; Cleis-
       thenes challenges; Megacles responds (*abac*).
(2c)   vii.8–11. Xerxes proposes; Mardonius accepts; Artabanus rejects;
       Xerxes reacts (*abca*).
       vii.140–141. Oracle predicts; Timon reacts with advice; Athenians con-
       sult; oracle repredicts (*abca*).

The third category is just about as near as Herodotus ever comes to a
true three-way dialogue:

(3)   viii.140–144. Alexander proposes; Spartans challenge; Athenians an-
       swer Alexander; Athenians answer Spartans (*abcc*).

It is worth noting that this dialogue is not only the most sophisticated
presentation of three-way confrontation in the *Histories* but it is also
the closest thing to such Thucydidean explications of underlying
causes and motivations as the Corinthian-Athenian-Spartan exchange in i.66–88. Indeed, there is sufficient similarity between the
two conferences to suggest the possibility of a rhetorical pattern if not
of actual influence: the first speaker in each case proposes a course of
action that is both tempting and apparently expedient (to medize and
win peace and freedom; to punish Athens and win respect and
power); the second speaker opposes the first, dwelling on the realities
and the rightness of the opposite course of action (to do your duty
and defend Greece; to mind your own business and arbitrate differences); in both conferences the people who are thus doubly challenged make two answers, one directed to the first speech (Athenian
rejection of Alexander's proposal; Spartan king's objection to Corinthian urging), the other to the second (Athenian reassurance of the
Spartans; Spartan ephor's rejection of Athenian advice). The chief
difference is between the united Athenian front in the Persian War
situation and the division in Spartan policy before the Peloponnesian
War. This difference may well result chiefly from the purposes of the
two historians in presenting the confrontations: Herodotus was concerned to show that it was the Athenians who held the key to victory
(for the Persians if they medized, for the Greeks if they held firm);
Thucydides' aim was apparently to present by means of both Archi-
damus' caution and Sthenelaidas' rashness the factors that made

Spartan success unlikely without Athenian cooperation and self-inflicted defeat.

The simplest three-speaker dialogues of pentad length involve two-stage pairs (speakers 1 and 2) with a reaction or conclusion by a third speaker:

v.51. Aristagoras proposes; Cleomenes temporizes; Aristagoras reproposes; Cleomenes retemporizes; Gorgo gives advice (*ababc*)

viii.26. A Persian asks; deserters answer; a Persian asks further; deserters answer further; Tritantaechmes concludes (*ababc*).

Even though in the former case the exchange is always only two-way (since Gorgo speaks only to her father), all three speakers are necessary, and this is emphasized in the first pair where Gorgo's presence is noted. In the latter case there is no real need for three speakers since Tritantaechmes could have been the original questioner, but certainly the effect of a third speaker drawing the conclusion is greater than if the questioner had followed through from his own questions.

The only other three-speaker pentad involves a change of scene as well as a shifting of pairs in a combination of one-way and two-way communication:

vii.14–18. Dream warns Xerxes; Xerxes asks Artabanus for help; Artabanus hesitates but agrees; Dream warns Artabanus; Artabanus advises Xerxes (*abcac*).

The dream's communications are only one-way, but they serve to evoke the two-way communication between Xerxes and Artabanus.

Two of the four three-speaker hexads show two-stage pairs (speakers 1 and 2) followed by a third pair (speakers 1 and 3):

iii.71–73. Darius challenges; Otanes responds; Darius challenges; Otanes responds; Darius challenges; Gobryas responds (*ababac*).

vii.234–237. Xerxes questions; Demaratus answers; Xerxes questions; Demaratus answers; Achaemenes challenges; Xerxes responds (*ababca*).

In both cases all three speakers are necessary so that the exchange will give both arguments against a particular course of action (first and second pairs) and motivation for it (third pair). Even though the third speaker must participate in the first two pairs to the extent of hearing what is said, all the exchanges are still basically only two-way.

The third speaker in another hexad plays a less vital role, taking a medial position rather than a final one and serving only to make possible two-stage question-and-answer pairs that will build up to the punchline:

vii.27–29. Pythius announces; Xerxes questions; Persians answer; Xerxes questions; Pythius answers; Xerxes concludes (*abcbab*).

The only other hexad with three speakers is really two two-speaker triads connected by their reduplicating subject matter. The exchanges are so completely two-way that in neither triad is the third speaker even a passive audience:

iii.27–28. Cambyses questions; governors answer; Cambyses reacts; Cambyses questions; priests answer; Cambyses reacts (*abaaca*).

The one heptad with three speakers is most comparable to the pentad in which the Dream serves as impetus and resource for the Xerxes-Artabanus exchange. Here the herald not only motivates the first question-and-answer pair but also must again be consulted to provide background for the final question-and-answer pair. The three speakers are all necessary but communication is still two-way:

iii.61–63. Herald announces; Cambyses questions Prexaspes, Prexaspes answers Cambyses; Prexaspes questions herald, herald answers Prexaspes; Cambyses questions Prexaspes, Prexaspes answers Cambyses (*abccabc*)

Three speakers are also present in the shifting scenes of the one nine-speech dialogue where again the third speaker is at first only passive audience to a two-way exchange. When he does become active it is not only to initiate a new two-way exchange but also to remove one of the original speakers from the scene before going on to a two-way exchange with the other, thus underlining the essentially two-speaker nature of the dialogue:

v.18–20. Persians challenge; Amyntas responds; Persians challenge; Amyntas responds; Alexander challenges; Amyntas responds; Alexander challenges; Persians respond; Alexander concludes (*ababcbcac*).

Only four other dialogues might be thought of as involving three speakers, and in no case is there any three-way communication. Either the dialogue itself or the third speaker is somewhat anomalous:

ii.115. Proteus questions; Paris answers; Proteus questions; Paris lies and servants speak; Proteus reacts (*abaca*).

iii.156. Babylonian guards question; Zopyrus answers; Babylonian magistrates question; Zopyrus answers (*abcb*).

v.92.z. Periander questions (through messenger); Thrasybulus answers (by action); Periander questions messenger; messenger answers (*abac*).

v.105. Darius asks; they answer; Darius prays and gives command; what servant is to say (*abac*).

This survey of the 35 dialogues in which more than two speakers take part demonstrates clearly the way in which pairs of speeches dominate the whole dialogue picture even when three or four speakers are of necessity involved. The strength of the pair has already been seen not only in the unexpectedly large number of tetrads made up of two-stage pairs but also in the predominance of pair composition in all of the dialogues from triads through decahexad.

As we have seen, the basic elements of discourse are the single speech and the pair, the combination of which produces the triad. But even more frequent than the triad is the combination of two interdependent pairs to make a tetrad. Such a combination of two pairs is often given added point by the conversion of the second pair into a triad, making a pentad. Other combinations of single speeches, pairs, and triads appear in hexads (most often three pairs or two triads but also a single plus pentad), heptads (triad and tetrad, etc.), and longer dialogues.

Appendix IV

Direct and Indirect Discourse

Comparative statistics will provide a basis for some conclusions concerning the use and meaning of direct and indirect quotation. Of the 861 speeches (including letters and oracles) considered in this study, 409 (47.5%) are quoted directly. A breakdown by categories will best show the distribution, but it should be noted that there was much subjectivity in the identification of the 85 indirectly quoted singles and to some extent also of the 51 pairs that are quoted indirectly. The figures, shown in Table 1, are to be regarded as rough approximations; they are not directly comparable to the figures for triads, tetrads, and longer dialogues.

The percentages of directly quoted speeches in the various categories are remarkably similar even if singles and pairs are included. All are within the 42–52% range except hexads and the longer dialogues, which should perhaps be exceptional: subjects that require so many

Table 1

		Speeches directly quoted	Percent of all speeches in category	Percent of all directly quoted speeches
177 singles	(177 speeches)	92	52%	22.5%
110 pairs	(220 speeches)	92	42%	22.5%
26 triads	(78 speeches)	37	47%	9%
47 tetrads	(188 speeches)	79	42%	19%
16 pentads	(80 speeches)	36	45%	9%
9 hexads	(54 speeches)	33	61%	8%
7 longer	(64 speeches)	40	63%	10%
Total	(861 speeches)	409		100%

Table 2

	All speeches quoted directly	Mixed quotation	All speeches indirectly quoted
177 single speeches	92 (52%)	—	85 (48%)
110 pairs	33 (30%)	26 (24%)	51 (46%)
26 triads	3 (12%)	21 (81%)	2 (7%)
47 tetrads	6 (13%)	27 (57%)	14 (30%)
16 pentads	2 (12.5%)	12 (75%)	2 (12.5%)
9 hexads	3 (33%)	4 (45%)	2 (22%)
7 longer dialogues	1 (14%)	6 (86%)	—

speeches must be of sufficient importance to be given the greater emphasis implied in direct quotation.* The fact that almost half of all directly quoted speeches appear either as singles or in pairs of speeches is perhaps reasonable, since only thus can a situation be dramatized and made vivid in brief compass. That the percentage of directly quoted speeches in tetrads is almost as great as that of singles or pairs results partly from the pair make-up of tetrads and partly from the exceptionally large number of tetrads.

The figures in Table 2 for all independent forms show that most dialogues are likely to have one or more speeches reported indirectly. The fact that both pairs and the other two forms that are mostly made up of pairs (tetrads and hexads) are less often mixed and more often indirectly quoted throughout than triads, pentads, and the longer dialogues may perhaps be explained by the often routine question-and-answer nature of pairs as opposed to the importance of conclusions drawn and punchlines spoken at the ends of triads and pentads. The significant percentage of mixed dialogues for all forms longer than pairs seems to reflect the fact that most scenes important enough to be dramatized include speeches that deserve the extra emphasis provided by direct quotation in an indirectly quoted context.

Since in addition to the independent forms listed above there are similar forms that go to make up longer dialogues and so are subordi-

---

*And if we exclude the decahexad with its fourteen indirectly quoted speeches from this last category (iii.21–23) because of its uniqueness, the percentage of directly quoted speeches in dialogues of seven, eight, nine, and ten speeches rises to 79% (38 of 48).

nate or dependent, figures on the direct, mixed, and indirect quotation of these should perhaps be compared (see Table 3). If we compare the percentages of the different kinds of quotation in independent and dependent forms, the results show some interesting features: dependent singles are more likely to be quoted directly than independent singles, presumably because so many of them are the concluding or punchline speeches of triads; the similarity of the percentages for independent and dependent pairs suggests that this most frequent and useful of all forms is least affected by the nature of its context, whether narrative or dialogue; the very considerable increase in the

Table 3*

Dependent forms	All speeches directly quoted	Mixed quotation	All speeches indirectly quoted
58 singles	40 (70%)	—	18 (30%)
203 pairs	67 (30%)	52 (26%)	84 (42%)
24 triads	7 (29%)	10 (42%)	7 (29%)
11 tetrads	3 (27%)	7 (64%)	1 (9%)
4 pentads	2 (50%)	2 (50%)	—
1 hexad	1 (100%)	—	—

* It is obvious that in this tabulation not only are the same speeches counted that were counted above in their independent forms but also many speeches are counted more than once. The dependent singles include 26 in 26 independent triads, 24 in dependent triads, and 8 in longer dialogues (i.86–87; iii.61–63, 140; v.73; vii.14–18, 27–29, 157–162; viii.137). Thus the 203 pairs include (a) 150 which are part of 26 independent triads, 47 tetrads, 11 pentads, 9 hexads, and 5 longer dialogues (26 plus 94 plus 11 plus 14 plus 5); (b) 24 which are part of the 24 dependent triads, 22 which make up the 11 dependent tetrads, 4 which are part of the 4 dependent pentads, and 3 which are part of the dependent hexad (24 plus 22 plus 4 plus 3). Similarly, the 24 dependent triads include not only 11 in independent pentads (i.90, 111–112; ii.115; iii.34–35; iv.114–115; v.49–50, 51, 105; vi.52; viii.26; ix.16), 2 in one independent hexad (iii.27–28), 1 each in independent heptad (i.158–159), ennead (v.18–19), and decad (vii.46–52), and 4 in the one decahexad (iii.21–23), but also 4 in 4 dependent pentads (i.88–89; vii.27–29, 46–52, 157–162). The 11 dependent tetrads are in 5 independent pentads (i.86–87; iii.140; v.73; vii.14–18; viii.137), 2 independent hexads (vii.101–104, 234–237), 1 heptad (i.158–159), 1 octad (i.30–32 made up of two tetrads), and 1 ennead (v.18–20). The 4 dependent pentads are in one heptad (i.88–89), and 2 hexads (vii.27–29, 157–162) and 1 decad (vii.46–52). The one dependent hexad is in a heptad (iii.61–63).

percentage of dependent triads, tetrads, pentads, and longer dialogues in which all speeches are directly quoted, on the other hand, reflects the greater importance of matters that give rise to lengthy discussion.

The arrangement of direct and indirect speeches within mixed dialogues can best be tested by figures for mixed pairs and triads (see Table 4), since these are the basic elements of longer dialogues as well as among the most frequent of exchanges. Again the independent and dependent pairs and triads are listed separately both as a cross-check and for comparison. What appears to be chiefly interesting here is the rarity of four of the six possible combinations for the triads, with 23 of 31 being either iiD or iDD, and only one other combination appearing more than twice. It is surely no coincidence that the three most used arrangements all end with a direct speech, and surely it is almost axiomatic that a direct speech is more emphatic than an indirect one. So it might have been thought obvious that a confrontation worth dramatizing in dialogue is likely to have a strong rather than a weak conclusion. But the fact that in the case of dependent mixed pairs those ending with an indirect speech (26) are just as numerous as their opposites (26) suggests that there may be other very real differences between pairs and triads than the number of speeches. Although such differences are most likely to be in content and function, form also plays a part, since pairs of speeches tend to be either question and answer or some kind of challenge and response. And it is

Table 4

26 independent	*indirect-Direct*	*Direct-indirect*
Mixed pairs:		
26 independent	18 (69%)	8 (31%)
52 dependent	26 (50%)	26 (50%)

	iiD	*iDD*	*iDi*	*DiD*	*DDi*	*Dii*
Mixed triads:						
21 independent	11 (52%)	5 (24%)	1	2	1	1
10 dependent	6 (60%)	1 (10%)		2	1	

obvious that in some situations it is the question or challenge that is more important, while in others it is the answer or response. That among independent pairs the number ending with a directly quoted speech is more than twice as great as those ending with one indirectly quoted suggests that a simple exchange in the midst of narrative is more likely to end emphatically, perhaps because it influences action.

Unlike pairs, which are compound, triads are complex, often in the form of thesis, antithesis, and synthesis, so that the first two elements are subordinated to the third. If from the point of view of content the third speech draws conclusions from the other two, it is equally true that with regard to function it is not the build-up but the crowning member that is likely to be effective in the narrative. Thus far, then, formal differences between pairs and triads in the use of direct and indirect speeches provide incentive for a close examination of the evidence for possible differences in both content and function.

Looking to tetrads, we find the figures shown in Table 5. Although the number of dependent tetrads is perhaps too small to be indicative, it does appear that they are more likely to be at least half directly quoted than are the independent tetrads. This may be explained, as was the difference between independent and dependent triads, by the relatively greater importance of subjects that the longer dialogues

Table 5

	4 direct	3 direct	2 direct	1 direct	0 direct
47 independent	6 (13%)	11 (23%) (4 DDDi, 4 DiDD, 3 iDDD)	6 (13%) (3 DiDi, 1 iiDD, 1 iDDi, 1 iDiD)	10 (21%) (5 iiiD, 3 iDii, 2 Diii)	14 (30%)
			49%		51%
11 dependent	3 (27%)	3 (27%) (1 iDDD, 1 DiDD, 1 DDiD)	2 (18%) (1 DDii, 1 iiDD)	2 (18%) (1 iDii, 1 iiDi)	1 (10%)
			72%		28%

illuminate and the consequent need for more emphasis. But it is also true that the longer the dialogue the harder it is to sustain the dramatic illusion in a succession of speeches in indirect quotation. The one exception in the *Histories* actually "proves" this rule, since the four indirectly quoted triads in iii.21–23 follow exactly the same form and have their impact through simple variations on the same theme rather than from any development or complication of thought.

As far as any tendency for direct statements to concentrate in one or more positions is concerned, tetrads are closer to pairs than to triads. That is, direct quotation of the final speech appears in 56% of the pairs and 90% of the triads, while in tetrads the percentage is 47%, which is even smaller than that for directly quoted speeches in the penultimate position (50%). Apparently it is the second pair of the two-stage tetrad that is emphasized by direct quotation, but not so regularly as in the last speech of a triad.

Pentads, on the other hand, show a final speech that is directly quoted in 80% of the examples, mostly perhaps because they are composed of pair and triad. The parallel between independent and dependent examples' use of direct and indirect quotation is shown in Table 6. Here again, and even more dramatically, it appears that the pentads in the longer dialogues have more directly quoted speeches than the independent forms.

Table 6

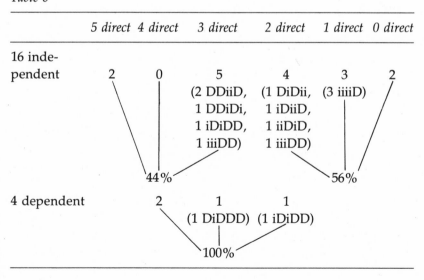

	5 direct	4 direct	3 direct	2 direct	1 direct	0 direct
16 independent	2	0	5 (2 DDiiD, 1 DDiDi, 1 iDiDD, 1 iiiDD)	4 (1 DiDii, 1 iDiiD, 1 iiDiD, 1 iiiDD)	3 (3 iiiiD)	2
			44%		56%	
4 dependent			2	1 (1 DiDDD)	1 (1 iDiDD)	
				100%		

The figures for hexads are presented in Table 7, in which it may be seen that 7 out of 10 have a final speech directly quoted.

One oddity in the reporting of speeches may suggest a criterion for the choice between direct and indirect quotation that has not yet been considered. A few speeches are begun in indirect discourse and continued in direct discourse (i.118, 125; iii.156.2–3; v.31; ix.2). In these cases it is regularly the background or scene-setting material at the beginning of the speech that is reported indirectly, with the command, appeal, or advice being given directly. The opposite arrangement appears in vii.5.2–3, where Mardonius gives advice in direct discourse and then Herodotus adds, "This speech urged vengeance, but he included also a parenthesis to the effect that Greece was a very beautiful country" and so on. In both combinations the directly quoted part of the speeches is that which has immediacy and relevance and is effective in the movement of the narrative. This kind of subordination may also operate in a dialogue where one or more speeches that have only incidental value are de-emphasized by being reported indirectly, thus setting off in high relief the directly quoted speeches.

Other criteria have already been mentioned in passing. The distinction between direct and indirect quotation may convey not only the relative importance and unimportance of what is said but also the relative importance and individuality of the person(s) speaking. Thus anonymous persons like heralds and ambassadors as well as undifferentiated groups are often quoted indirectly; strong personalities,

Table 7

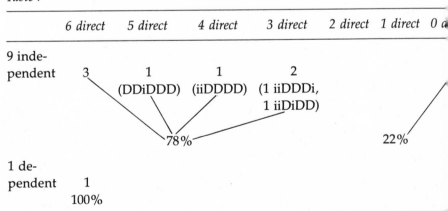

	6 direct	5 direct	4 direct	3 direct	2 direct	1 direct	0 d
9 independent	3	1 (DDiDDD)	1 (iiDDDD)	2 (1 iiDDDi, 1 iiDiDD)			
			78%			22%	
1 dependent	1 100%						

on the other hand, are both reflected and exemplified in direct quotation. Directly quoted answers or confrontations that are effective in the narrative are very often introduced by questions or challenges that are indirectly quoted. This is particularly notable in the case of questions to oracles where the contrast in interest and importance to the narrative is reflected in the indirect reporting of the question and the direct quotation of the oracle. Similarly, punchlines stand out more boldly if they are quoted directly after a build-up of indirect discourse. Elsewhere, too, a build-up of interest and tension is achieved by a change from indirect quotation to direct; see for example various two-stage tetrads and three-stage hexads where the first pair is frequently indirect.

Indirect quotation of first speeches and parenthetic speeches in otherwise directly quoted dialogues is thus reasonable and understandable. But a special explanation is required when in such a dialogue the last speech is indirectly quoted, since the usual case is that this is quite literally the "final word" which motivates or explains some action in the narrative. Such de-emphasized final speeches regularly occur when the directly quoted penultimate speech is a compelling command or appeal which fulfills the dialogue's motivating or explaining function and to which the only response is simple acquiescence (e.g., i.8–9; iii.68–69, 85; iv.114–115; vi.129–130).

Another sort of difference between speeches quoted directly and indirectly results from the extent to which the speaker has to hand a ready-made rhetoric that may be applied to the particular situation. If such arguments are available, direct quotation is most likely, partly because of the probable length of such a speech and partly because of the ease and handiness of the material. What appear from their frequency in the *Histories* to be rhetorical commonplaces of this sort are the following: in making a case for military aggrandizement the glory-duty-ease-and-booty formula may be tailored to a variety of situations; in advising restraint or caution there is frequent employment of either the divine jealousy theme or insistence on the need for wise counsel. (For other commonplaces see Chapter 4). The responses to such generalized forms of persuasion are likely to be more particular to the situation and, because they are less likely to have ready-made themes that are applicable, will often be both shorter and indirectly quoted.

Notes

1. Narrative Transitions

1. See the works listed in the bibliography by: Aly, Cobet, Egermann, Erbse, Fornara, Fränkel, van Groningen (1953, 1958), Immerwahr (1954, 1956, 1956/7, 1966), Jacoby, Kazazis, Lattimore, Myres, Pohlenz, Regenbogen, Wood.

2. Stith Thompson, *Tales of the North American Indians* (Bloomington, Ind., 1929), p. 333.

3. Ella E. Clark, *Indian Legends of the Pacific Northwest* (Berkeley, Calif., 1953), p. 151.

4. Cf. *Iliad* 1.1–5 and *Odyssey* 1.1–9.

5. Cf. *Iliad* 1.6–7 and *Odyssey* 1.10.

6. If it is asked why the Atys story is "on the way" to the cause of the conflict between Greeks and Persians, the answer must involve other aspects of Herodotus' composition besides pure structure, such as his moral bias, the pressure of relevance, and the influence of tragedy.

7. Immerwahr (1966), pp. 42–45, 59–78.

8. See Herodotus' use of the word *hodos* as "path of discourse": i.95.1, 117.2; ii.20.1, 22.1.

9. Cf. Hdt. iv.30.1: "Since my account has from the beginning invited digressions, I admit to surprise that nowhere in Elis can mules be born." Cf. vii.171.1

10. Geographical digressions similarly follow mention of someone going somewhere so that they set the scene and feed into his arrival, e.g., Cappadocia in i.72 between i.71.1 and i.73.1. The placement of the longer ethnographic logoi directly after Persian attention is turned upon a potential new conquest has long been recognized as similarly scene-setting, e.g., i.178–187, i.201–204; ii.2–182, and so on.

11. Immerwahr (1966), pp. 306–326.

12. Divining purpose from result is certainly a Herodotean habit, related presumably to the tendency to "look to the end" that characterizes both Solon's philosophy and Herodotus' narrative method. That is, the historian's knowledge of where he is going tends to "inform" the narrative of the whole journey. So, having stated his subject, he takes aim at it by seeking out the

path that will lead directly to it. Where the subject is the result of an action, for instance, the most direct path will start from a purpose that is conditioned and defined by the result—e.g., i.86–87, where the rescue of Croesus by Apollo suggests one possible purpose: Cyrus' putting him on the pyre to see if the god would rescue him.

13. See M. L. West, *Hesiod Works and Days* (Oxford, 1978), pp. 41–46.

14. See van Groningen (1958), pp. 57–61, where such topic sentences removing suspense are regarded as a literary device and due to general Greek preference.

15. More complex is the forward spiraling of Croesus' action against Cyrus: the intention in i.46 serves to introduce the testing of oracles and its aftermath, with renewed intention in i.71 that introduces both warning and start of expedition (and geographical digression), with renewed motivation in i.73 that introduces a historical digression, and a final summing up of motivations before the arrival at the Halys River in i.75. Compare the Scythians' intentions and approaches to the Ionians in iv.120–142. The epic parallel is seen in the two divine assemblies in *Odyssey* 1 and 5.

16. Compare the way in which in the *Odyssey* Theoclymenus' genealogy is tucked in between his arrival and the confrontation with Telemachus (15.225–255), which is paralleled in turn by the account of Phocaean voyaging to Tartessos tucked between Harpagus' arrival to besiege Phocaea and his attack on the city walls, which had been built by means of Tartessian wealth (i.163–165).

17. This chronology is Herodotus' own, and this interpretation applies whether or not the Themistocles decree from Troizen is genuine.

18. Much of the argument concerning the relation between the Themistocles decree from Troizen and Herodotus' account could have been avoided if the nature of this digression had been properly appreciated. For a summary statement of the arguments and bibliography see C. Hignett, *Xerxes' Invasion of Greece* (Oxford, 1963), pp. 458–468.

The most recent treatment is that of N. G. L. Hammond, *JHS* 102 (1982), 75–93. Hammond uses a Herodotean pluperfect to date the Herodotean version of the "Themistocles decree" and the oracles that preceded it to a time before the meeting at the Isthmus. This contradicts his earlier perception that in Book vii "the topics follow one another like beads on a string, each topic being clearly marked off from the next one . . . the end of a topic is usually marked by *men dē* or *men* in its final clause" (p. 75) and "while this . . . keeps each topic clear to the listener, it leaves the chronological relationship between the topics vague; for the topics follow one another as topics and not as consecutive steps in a chronological sequence" (p. 76). And yet, when in vii.145 Herodotus concludes the topic of the oracles and decree with "*ta men dē chrēstēria tauta toisi Athēnaioisi egegonee,*" Hammond argues on the basis of the *egegonee* for a clear chronological connection between the oracles-and-decree and the council at the Isthmus reported in the following sentence. The notion that the pluperfect must provide a chronological connection of this sort does not take into account what seems to be a feature of the oral, run-on style in which after a digression, in rejoining the main narrative, it is necessary to remind the audience of what had sparked the digression. The *egegonee* here seems to be such a "narrative pluperfect." That is, after reporting the oracles and Athenian reaction in vii.140–143, Herodotus digresses to tell of Themistocles' earlier shipbuilding, the need for more ships, and the decision after debate on the oracle to meet the Persians at sea; then follows what Hammond calls the final clause of a topic marked by *men dē:* "these oracles then had been given to the Athenians." Thus the pluperfect reverts to what had introduced the shipbuilding and decree and puts a period to that digression. What makes this passage more complicated is that the oracles themselves are very much a part of a longer digression in which due credit is given to Athens for spearheading resistance to the Persians. That is, the mainline narrative detailing general Greek reaction to the Persian threat is interrupted after vii.138 so that Herodotus may express his personal opinion about the Athenian role in saving Greece even despite discouragement from Delphi. Only in 145 is the main-line narrative resumed with the Council at the Isthmus, and there is no indication whatsoever as to the date of either the oracles or the decree, both of which are tied only to the defence of Athens and float free in time.

19. Other examples of time-filling digressions include: i.125.3–4 (list of Persian tribes between Cyrus' summons and their arrival); i.142–151 (account of Ionians and Aeolians between sending of messengers to Sparta and their arrival); iii.28.2 (account of Apis between Cambyses' sending the priests to bring him and their bringing); almost any other sending of messengers to persons or places unknown.

20. Background material is inserted in the story itself only when it is new and hitherto untouched in the narrative. To have inserted here the story of how Democedes happened to be in Susa would have meant looking backward in a way foreign to the oral style. The only exception that occurs to me is the Arion story (i.23–24), which is a digression not inserted in the story that gives rise to it but saved till after the end of the story; that, however, is because of its irrelevance to the story.

21. Other examples of hooks include: i.80.3 (Cyrus' command not to kill Croesus so that when in i.85.3 his dumb son identifies him by crying out, "Do not kill Croesus," no explanation is needed); i.110.1 (Mitradates' wife is given her "canine" name to prepare for the story put about by Cyrus' parents of his having been suckled by a bitch in i.122.3); and i.123.2 (Harpagus persuades disaffected Medes to support Cyrus in preparation both for his letter promising their aid, i.124.3, and the action, i.127.3).

22. It is interesting here to compare M. L. West on heroic poetry (*Hesiod Works and Days*, p. 43): "It already has a certain structure, because the story itself depends upon a particular sequence of critical events. A further structuring is given by established poetic technique. If a battle is to be described, for instance, the poet has at his disposal an array of conventional ingredients from which to construct his narrative." Herodotus had little in the way of conventional ingredients for his historical battles, but his accounts are rich in

anecdotes of events both before and after a battle which, in their attachment to the battle, need no other structural justification.

23. Cf. ps. Plutarch, *de Herodoti malignitate* 22, where Antenor and Dionysius of Chalcis are given as references for the rescue of the Corcyrean boys by the Cnidians rather than the Samians, so that this at least should not have been a cause of long-lasting enmity between Corinth and Samos.

24. The examples given here are limited to Book i and so do not include all possible varieties.

25. This is the only time in Book i when a particular source is thus referred to; the regular form is "the Corinthians [e.g.] say . . ." When the source is not identified the usual form is simply *legetai*. How and why then do the four uses of *punthanomai* differ from the situations in which *legetai* appears? It is likely that *punthanomai* indicates that a special inquiry was made, whereas *legetai* is used of unsolicited information.

26. For example, there are thirty-nine participles of *punthanomai* in the first four books of the *Histories*; five of these (i.54.1, 135; ii.49.2, 91.6; iii.12.1) serve merely to explain how the new knowledge affected the subsequent action; in the other thirty-four cases the new knowledge appears in and of itself to be the cause of the action (i.20, 52, 69.1, 70.2, 86.2, 96.3, 97.1, 152.1, 153.1, 155.1, 157.1, 212.1; ii.13.3, 30.4, 44.1, 113.3, 121e3, 162.1, 162.3; iii.7.2, 16.6, 25.7, 48.2, 58.4, 119.5, 127.1, 134.5, 151.1, 154.1; iv.80.2, 134.1, 152.1, 166.1, 167.2). This count does not include numerous cases in which a finite form of the verb is used in a temporal clause with much the same meaning as that of the participle. Much the same kind of statistics could be gathered for each of the other verbs.

27. The ubiquity of *gar* in the *Histories* (some 1,479 instances in about 800 pages average out to almost two on every page, although many pages have as many as four or five) is evidence of the historian's readiness to explain. To what extent this readiness is a result or in anticipation of audience reactions is, of course, impossible to say, but it seems likely to be considerable.

2. Patterns of Discourse

1. See R. Barthes, "Historical Discourse," in *Introduction to Structuralism*, ed. M. Lane (New York, 1970), p. 155: "The paradox comes full circle: narrative structure was evolved in the crucible of fiction (via myth and the first epics), yet it has become at once the sign and the proof of reality. It is clear that the attenuation (if not disappearance) of narrative in contemporary historians, who deal in structures rather than chronology, implies much more than a change of school; it represents in fact a fundamental ideological transformation; historical narrative is dying; from now on the touchstone of history is not so much reality as intelligibility." Also P. Munz, "History and Myth," *Philosophical Quarterly* 6 (1956), 6: "The facts, in other words, are loose. They are not necessarily worked loose by the imagination of a mythmaker. On the contrary, if we analyze the matter sufficiently, we will find that

the only structural attachment facts have is the one provided for them by a pattern of myth, that is, by a story which is itself not based upon simple observation of historical facts in a certain order."

2. It might be that the very few speeches introduced by *toiade* or the equivalent (less than 3% of the total; see Appendix III) are evidence of variety in the tradition from which Herodotus is making a selection, but there is no case in which alternate speeches are given. For another suggestion concerning the use of *toiade*, see Appendix III.

3. In other words, even before Thucydides made it explicit Herodotus was consulting *ta deonta* in the composition of speeches.

4. For recent work that has been done see the following in the bibliography: Aly (1929), Comparini, Deffner, Fränkel, Heni, Hohti, Jacoby, Kennedy, Lohmann, Pohlenz, Robertson, Schulz, Solmsen, Waters.

5. See the bibliography: Barthes, Dray, Finley, Gardiner, Goody, Louch, Mandelbaum, Munz, Porter, White (1978).

6. The line to be drawn between speeches quoted indirectly and reported as narrative is difficult to draw. See Appendix II for examples.

7. See Appendix II for listing of speeches and dialogues and Appendix III for a survey of formal aspects.

8. If we look to Homer for precedents and parallels to Herodotean single speeches, perhaps the fifty-two that are found in *Iliad* 1–5 provide an adequate sample. Although the form, content, and function of many of these are more complex than simple, they do fall into the following general categories of content: command, advice, appeal (including prayer), and announcement (that is, statement of fact or attitude). In each case the reference is to the first line of the speech only: fifteen speeches of command (1.321, 334; 2.8, 110, 157, 173, 200, 796; 3.82, 130; 4.193, 204, 234, 242, 509); nine speeches of advice (2.23, 190, 434; 4.93; 5.347, 440, 472, 529, 601); seventeen speeches of appeal (1.36, 451, 573, 586; 2.412; 3.250, 276, 297, 320, 350; 5.31, 109, 358, 455, 464, 684, 714); eleven speeches of announcement (1.442; 3.156, 304, 365, 456; 4.82, 285; 5.102, 421, 428, 787). For the most part, speeches of command, appeal, prayer, and advice serve to motivate action on the part of others, but there are cases where these speeches are not heeded or where the requested action is not reported. In both these situations the speech is either a means of pointing up the lack of action or it is an end in itself, explaining and characterizing the situation or the speaker. Speeches of announcement, on the other hand, are almost invariably ends in themselves either as reaction (for example, the Trojan elders' comment on Helen's effect on them, 3.156) or as explanations of the speaker's own action (for example, 1.442, Odysseus' formal statement of delivery, on handing Chryseis over to her father). The parallel between Homeric and Herodotean single speeches seems to be remarkably close in content and function; the almost invariably direct form of Homeric speeches contrasts with the large number of indirectly quoted utterances in the *Histories*.

9. The fifty-eight include eight which by serving as introductions to pattern tetrads, pentads, and hexads convert them to pentads, hexads, and

heptads; the fifty, on the other hand, join with pairs to make up triads. Of these fifty triads twenty-six are independent and twenty-four are part of longer dialogues. Many of these dependent singles are quoted indirectly but parallel in content the directly quoted independent singles listed in Appendix II.

10. Homeric parallels may be found in the twenty-two pairs of speeches that appear in *Iliad* 1–9. By and large the first speeches of these pairs have much the same form and content as the Homeric single speeches, that is, command, advice, appeal (including prayer), and announcement; a few have form and content not appropriate for single speeches, that is, questions that require answers and challenges that evoke counterchallenges. It is the second speech of a pair that determines the function of the dialogue, since the function of the first speech is more or less limited to evoking the second speech. If the second speech is a simple rejection of the preceding appeal or advice, the dialogue is itself a kind of action and end in itself which may also serve to block a possible line of action (1.17; 5.243; 6.407; 7.96; 8.201, 281). The same is true of a challenge or announcement that counters the preceding challenge or announcement (5.284, 633; 6.518; 7.226). Only pairs in which the second speech is complex seem to motivate action; sometimes the preceding appeal, advice, or command is accepted but with a proviso or amendment that somewhat redirects the impetus of the first speech (2.56; 3.39, 86; 4.257; 5.115; 8.352); sometimes the preceding appeal, advice, or command is rejected and a new proposal is made that gives rise to the following action (3.427; 5.872; 6.253; 7.446). The two questions are answered with either information or encouragement to act that serves to motivate (5.757; 6.376). Homeric paired speeches are thus seen to have much the same content and function as Herodotean pairs except for the much larger role played in the *Histories* by question-and-answer pairs. The reason for this is obvious, since the communication of information necessarily is both more important and more frequent in Herodotus' panoramic narrative than on the battlefield at Troy.

11. Pairs of speeches are not only the most numerous of all independent dialogues but also the most frequent and useful element in longer dialogues. In addition to the 110 independent pairs catalogued in Appendix II (33 direct, 26 mixed, 51 indirect), the following number of dependent pairs occur in combination:

26 in 26 independent triads plus	23 in 24 dependent triads
94 in 47 independent tetrads plus	22 in 11 dependent tetrads
11 in 11 independent pentads plus	4 in 4 dependent pentads
14 in 6 independent hexads plus	3 in 1 dependent hexad
5 in 4 longer dialogues	
150	52

The 312 pairs (110 independent and 202 dependent) should be compared with the total number of single speeches—that is, 235 (92 direct, 85 indirect, 58 dependent)—to show that the pair is the more frequent unit of discourse in both independent and dependent use. If we compare the total number of speeches in 312 pairs (624) with the 235 singles, it appears that the number of paired speeches is almost three times that of singles. And if we compare the 202 dependent pairs with the 58 dependent singles, it is even more obvious that dialogue is based on give and take, as surely must have been expected.

12. *Il.* 1.202*; 3.162*, 192*; 5.373; 6.123; 7.24; 9.673; 10.159, 303; 11.816. The starred examples are part of longer dialogues. In all cases only the first line is given.

13. All seventeen are independent. Six have three speakers instead of the usual two; these are indicated by "(3)." *Il.* 2.225 (3), 284 (3); 3.390; 4. 155. 303, 338, 370 (3); 5.800; 7.279, 348 (3), 385 (3); 8.5, 139, 447; 9.17 (3), 96; 10.234.

14. The ten tetrads in Books 1–12 are as follows (the four that are starred are part of longer dialogues): Two-stage, 1.106*, 352, 503, 540; 4.7*; 5.171; 10.37, 82*. Chiastic, i.59*. Other, 6.326.

15. I have argued this in the case of the Ionian Revolt, the failure of which seems to have colored Herodotus' view of its initiators' purpose and actions: *Historia* 17 (1968), 69–82. See also objection thereto by K. H. Waters, *Historia* 19 (1970), 504–508.

16. Hdt. i.67, 116.3–5; iii.51, 130.1–2; vi. 69.2.

17. Hdt. iii.38; vi. 86g.

18. Hdt. iii.155; iv.155; v.92z; vii.38–39.

19. Hdt. iii.156; iv. 145; v.82.

20. Two of the question-and-answer examples are not readily accounted for either as explicating and underlining general historical forces or as explaining particular actions: i.119.5–7 (Astyages and Harpagus) and iii.119.3–6 (Darius and the wife of Intaphernes). Both of these have a kind of independence in that they are recorded more for their own sake than as an explanation of something else. The whole narrative in each case (of Astyages' revenge on Harpagus and of Darius' reaction to Intaphernes' conspiracy) seems to have no other function than to lead up to the dialogues, which have an anecdotal quality complete with final punchline that makes them irresistible even though they have little relevance to the narrative as a whole. That anecdotes of this sort have the same format as realistic dialogues of motivation is evidence of the pattern's strength and relevance.

21. Some merely illuminate the narrative without being closely tied in: i.129, 152–153; ii.160; vi.50; viii.88; ix.90–91. Others are an integral part of some larger whole: i.37–40; viii.140–144; ix.109.

22. See Appendix II, Other Tetrads.

23. This pentad could also be viewed as a directly quoted triad (speeches 1, 2, and 5) interrupted by an indirectly quoted pair (speeches 3 and 4), the parenthetical nature of which is indicated by the indirect quoting. The effect is somewhat that of a triad with an internal footnote. But the resultant pentad does emphasize the extent to which Herodotean dialogues move in a step-by-step fashion, leaving nothing to the imagination.

24. That the pair-triad combination is here the dominant one (rather than the tetrad-single) is suggested by the fact that both pair and triad end

with long and discursive directly quoted speeches with the indirectly quoted question, challenge, and response serving primarily to lead up to them. The synthesizing feature of Spako's last speech involves a restatement of her challenge combined with an answer to the objection raised in Mitradates' response.

25. The second of this sort is *Il.* 10.82. The third Homeric pentad comes at the end of the long dialogue (a decahexad) in Book I (173) by which the break between Agamemnon and Achilles is accomplished; see below, Appendix II, Triad-Pair Pentads.

26. See Appendix II, Single-Tetrad Pentads.

27. Note that the order in which the three parts of the second question are answered is reversed (*xyz–zyx*), providing a good example of *hysteron proteron Homerikōs*.

28. A second hexad in the first half of the *Iliad* is part of a longer dialogue: 10.383.

29. The one octad in *Iliad* 1–12 (3.162) is made up as follows: triad/triad/pair.

30. The one ennead in *Iliad* 1–12 (10.370) is made up of pair, hexad, single. The apparently abrupt ending emphasizes the way in which Dolon is cut down just as he was about to speak.

31. Compare the one decahexad in *Iliad* 1–12: 1.59, which is made up of two tetrads and a pentad interrupted by a triad. See above, note 25.

32. The four triads in which the king is both questioner and reactor divide neatly into two pairs: the first pair points up the deceptiveness and "weakness" of the Persians; the second pair starts with an echo of the first but then, after the king's approval of the wine, introduces a different kind of question and answer, the reaction to which hints again at the weakness of the Persians and so evokes the question of the final pair.

3. How Could Herodotus Imitate Homer?

1. For ancient discussions see Aristotle, *Rhet.* 3.18 (1419a); Demetrius, *Eloc.* 279; Cicero, *de orat.* 3.53, 203; *Rhet. ad Herennium* IV.xv.22; Quintilian 9.2.7–16, 9.3.98; "Longinus" *de sublim.* 18.

2. Variants of this question occur at *Il.* 9.273; 11.299; 16.692.

3. *Il.* 2.484, and variants in 11.218; 14.508; 16.112.

4. That is, the author of *peri eroteseos kai apokriseos,* a paraphrase with commentary of Aristotle, *Rhet.* 3.18, who is unknown. See the text in L. Spengel, *Rhet. Gr.,* 1.163–168, or in *Rh. Mus.* 5 (1947), 261–266.

5. J. G. Genung, *The Working Principles of Rhetoric* (Boston, 1900), p. 97; cf. Longinus, *de sublim.* 18.1.

6. This number is necessarily approximate since definition is not easy: whether, for example, a question asking for information that it does not elicit is rhetorical or not. Omitted from this number are both soliloquy questions

(e.g., 11.404, 17.97) and the half-exclamatory questions like "What sort of word have you spoken?" (e.g., 1.552; 4.350).

7. Again definition is often a matter of interpretation. The list includes the following: 1.365, 414; 2.225, 323; 4.31, 351; 5.421, 757, 872; 6.145, 254; 8.140, 293, 413, 447; 9.77, 337, 437; 10.432; 11.656, 666, 792, 838; 13.275; 14.43, 333; 15.130, 403; 16.441, 721, 859, 17.327, 450, 475; 18.6, 287, 364, 429; 19.56, 81, 90, 227, 420; 20.87, 297, 332; 21.153, 394; 22.179; 23.94, 458, 670; 24.33, 90, 128, 201, 239, 362. Also the two-question combinations in note 9 below.

8. The complete list is: i.37.2–3, 109.4, 155.1; iii.73.1, 80.3, 81.2, 82.5*, 151.2; iv.80.3, 118.2*; vi.12.3, 97.2; vii.9al*, 9g, 50.2; viii.68.a2*, 106.3, 140a3; ix.58.1, 122.2. The starred examples are those with two-question combinations described below.

9. Examples in addition to *Il.* 1.202 and 14.264 are 9.338; 17.443; 20.178; 21.106.

10. The complete list includes the following: 1.150, 291; 2.174, 194, 339; 3.46, 399*; 4.242*, 371; 5.171, 349, 465*, 473, 633; 6.55*; 7.24*; 8.94, 352; 10.159*; 12.244, 409; 13.219, 810; 14.88, 364, 471; 15.18, 440, 504, 553; 16.31, 422, 627; 17.170, 469, 586; 20.83, 184, 188; 21.369, 474, 481; 23.474. The starred examples are those with two-question combinations.

11. Cf. the "biographies" of Cambyses and Cleomenes as well as the presentation of the Ionian Revolt.

12. For the view that the two episodes to which these questions belong were designed to frame the *Histories*, see E. Wolff, "Das Weib der Masistes," *Hermes* 92 (1964), 51–58.

13. The following four examples all use the two-question combination by which the second (and third) question narrows the range and makes more specific the thrust of the first question to make the speaker's point.

14. Cf. Grimm, no. 94, "The Clever Peasant Girl," and *Motif-index of Folk-literature* (Stith Thompson, *Indiana Studies*, Bloomington, Ind., 1955–58), J 1200–1600.

15. Similar in its repetition of steps 3 and 4 is the episode of Croesus on the pyre (i.86–87). Variants in which there are both double or triple questioning and other differences are i.88–89; v.12–13; vii.27.

4. Look to the End

1. Comparable simple alternatives are i.91.4 and iv.9.4. In the former the oracle explains that Croesus should have asked whether his own kingdom or that of Cyrus was meant; no answer is needed since the narrative has already revealed that the first alternative was operative. In iv.9.4 the Snake-woman asks Heracles about the sons she will bear him, whether to settle them in Scythia or send them to him; he tells her to settle the one who passes the test she is to set and banish the others.

2. See also iii.32.3, 53.3; v.49.8, 92eta5; vi.48.1; vii.205.3. Alone of these vi.48.1 and vii.205.3 are not dialogue but narrative: in the first Darius was

testing what the Greeks had in mind, whether to fight or to surrender. This is a narrative question, and the narrative answers first with those who surrendered and then, by way of Aeginetan-Athenian enmity, with those who would fight. The second is similar. This narrative use of alternatives is reminiscent of the Homeric *ei mē* construction by means of which the poet takes note of two possibilities: what would have happened if someone had not done something and what actually did happen.

    3. The other three are ii.114.2; v.124.2; viii.36.1. Of these the first and last simply use the two obvious choices to prepare for the less obvious third. In v.124.2 Hecataeus plays the role of wise adviser, and his rejection of Aristagoras' two alternatives serves to justify Aristagoras' failure and death when he chooses one of them.

    4. This dictum seems to have been applied by Herodotus not only to speeches presented to clarify issues but also to variant accounts which he records so that the reader may make an informed choice on the basis of the evidence. See, for example, iii.122.1: "These two causes of Polycrates' death are reported; it is possible to believe whichever one wishes." Cf. v.45.2 and vi.137.1.

    5. Although there are full-dress confrontations between two speakers for and against a particular undertaking, there are also situations in which the impetus for an action is not a speech, but it is still countered by a warning. Aside from the Mardonius–Artabanus exemplification of the *peitho* tragic warner confrontation (vii.9–10), there are these other juxtaposed speeches for and against an action the failure of which seems to stem from the refusal to accept the warning: i.8, Candaules vs. Gyges; iii.122–124, Oroetes vs. Polycrates' daughter; v.35–36, Histiaeus and Hecataeus. Examples in which the impetus for the undertaking is more a matter of narrative than of speech include the following: i.71 (after Croesus was led on by unthinking acceptance of an ambiguous oracle, Sandanis warned against attacking the Persians); i.206–207 (after Persian nobles advised accepting Tomyris' offer and receiving the Massagetae into Persia, Croesus warned against thinking immortal thoughts; this warning was unheeded but his practical advice was accepted, and because Cyrus again refused to heed Tomyris' warning in i.212, led to Cyrus' death); iv.83 (Darius' eagerness to conquer Scythia and take vengeance for the earlier invasion of Persian territory was countered by Artabanus' warning, unsuccessfully); viii.68 (other advisers all urged Xerxes to fight a sea battle; Artemisia spoke in warning against it, unsuccessfully).

    6. See i.37–39; iv.126; vii.160–161; viii.134.2. Of these simple choices presented without moral or practical evaluation and without description of potential results, only three (i.11, 37, 206) serve to introduce and motivate action, and they do so only by means of the answering speech or speeches. The others are all concerned either in themselves or in their answers to explain or clarify already existing situations or attitudes. Two other simple choices are offered, but since neither is taken up the order is immaterial and the presentation seems to be included in the proposal more for the sake of the pattern than for any function it fulfills. In ix.26.6 the Tegeates conclude their claim by magnanimously offering to let the Spartans choose which wing they

are to command. This is immediately followed by the Athenian speech so that the only choice the Spartans make is between Tegeates and Athenians. In ix.48.4 Mardonius challenges the Spartans to a "duel" and offers a choice, if they accept, whether the others should then fight or whether the outcome of the duel will be definitive. Since the challenge is not accepted, there can be no choice and the offer of alternatives is apparently only an expected part of the proposal pattern.

7. One speech provides a kind of transition from the group of simple and open choices to these slanted speeches: Mardonius offers Xerxes a choice (viii.100.3) between immediately attempting the Peloponnesus or waiting, but before Xerxes can choose, Mardonius goes on to urge a third possibility— that Xerxes leave him to continue the war. It is this last course that Xerxes pairs with the attack on the Peloponnesus when he consults his other gener- als and Artemisia: Mardonius urges me to attempt the Peloponnesus or he wishes me to leave him 30,000 men to finish the war. Artemisia's answer takes up the latter alternative and never returns to the former, presumably because this allows a direct transition to Xerxes' decision to accept her advice and his consequent action.

8. See i.212.3; iv.118; vi.11; vii.236; viii.140. In all these speeches the use of alternatives backed by their potential for good and evil serves both to provide arguments for and against the two courses of action and to define the issues at stake and so to clarify the situation. The order in which the alterna- tives and their potential results are presented depends as much on the use of the speech as a means of transition as it does on the speech's persuasive function. Whether the promise of goods or the warning of evils may be most effective is also an important influence on the order of argument, since a final threat may sometimes seem the most significant motivating factor while at other times the clinching argument may be a vision of freedom and prosperity.

9. Other choices that simply present two possibilities to be considered in making a decision are presented in i.207.1–2; vi.86al; vii.10theta; viii.102. Most of these involve warnings which, being unheeded, prefigure and justify a coming disaster.

10. If proverbs are limited to "metaphors from one species to another" (according to Aristotle, *Rhet.* 3.11.14) comparatively few of the sayings used by Herodotus are true proverbs. They do, however, give trenchant expression to what we call proverbial sentiments, and so the words "proverb" and "maxim" will be used almost interchangeably here.

11. Others are: i.5.4, 32.1, 207.2; iii.40.2, 43.1, 52.5, 53.4 (bis); v.24.3; vi.37.2; vii.10d2, 10e, 49.3, 152.2.

12. Others are: i.32.9, 91.1; iii.36.1, 65.3, 72.2, 81.3, 134.2; vi.86d; vii.9g, 10e, 16a, 50.2 (bis), 51.1, 104.2, 157.3; viii.60g; ix.16.4.

13. That is, i.8.2, 87.4, 120.3; iii.53.4 (bis), 80.3, 127.2, 134.3; vi.11.2; vii.10eta2, 11.3, 172.3; ix.16.4.

14. That is, i.8.3, 32.4, 207.1; ii.120.5; vi.1.2; vii.49.5, 162.1, 237.3; viii.59.1 (bis).

15. vii.46.4, 49.4.

16. *Greek Proverbs*. Göteborgs Kungl. Veternskaps- och Vitterhets-Samhälles Handlingar, Sjätte Följden, Ser. A. Band 4. No. 8 (Göteborg, 1954), p. 9.

17. *Proverbs, Sentences and Proverbial Phrases from English Writings Mainly before 1500* (Harvard, 1968), p. xiv.

18. His statement (iv.205) that the gods caused Pheretime's horrible death because they found her style of vengeance *epiphthonos* is not relevant, partly because the compound form of the adjective involves more resentment than jealousy and partly because Herodotus certainly does not imply that Pheretime was assuming divine prerogatives.

19. These last two are reminiscent of Hector's line to Andromache (6.488): "I think that no one of men has escaped fate."

20. Compare two Homeric maxims concerned with counsel: "Good is the persuasion of a friend" (*Il.* 11.793 equals 15.404); "The minds of the noble can be turned" (*Il.* 15.203).

21. The other three are iii.81.3; vii.51.1; viii.60g.

22. Others are iii.53.4, 134.2; vi.86d; vii.104.2.

23. Of the possible 74, the following 31 have not been included in text or notes: i.32.8, 74.4, 87.4, 96.2, 120.3; ii.120.5; iii.53.4 (bis), 72.2, 80.3, 134.3; vii.10eta2, 11.3, 18.2, 39.1, 46.2, 49.4, 49.5, 50.1, 50.2, 50.3, 152.2, 160.1, 237.3; viii.68g, 102.1, 142.5; ix.16.4, 17.4, 54.1, 122.3.

24. Hesiod had changed Homer's "A fool learns when the thing is done" (*Il.* 17.32) to "Having suffered the fool learns" (*WD* 218).

Selected Bibliography

Aly, W. "Formprobleme der frühen griechischen Prosa," *Philologus* Supp. 21.3 (1929).

—— "Herodots Sprache," *Glotta* 15 (1926), 84–117.

Barthes, Roland, "Historical Discourse," in *Introduction to Structuralism*, ed. Michael Lane, pp. 145–155. New York, 1970.

Beck, I. *Die Ringkomposition bei Herodot und ihre Bedeutung für die Beweistechnik.* (*Spudasmata* XXV.) Hildesheim, 1971.

Cobet, J. *Herodots Exkurse und die Frage der Einheit seines Werkes.* (*Historia* Einzelschr. 17.) Wiesbaden, 1971.

Colby, B., and Cole, M. "Culture, Memory and Narrative," in *Modes of Thought*, ed. R. Horton and R. Finnegan, pp. 63–91. London, 1973.

Comparini, B. *Peitho in Herodotean Speeches.* (Ph.D. dissertation, Yale University, 1970.) University Microfilms, Ann Arbor, Michigan, 1977.

Deffner, August. *Die Rede bei Herodot und ihre Weiterbildung bei Thukydides.* Munich, 1933.

Dorson, R. M. "Oral Styles of American Folk Narrative," in *Style in Language*, ed. T. A. Sebeok, pp. 27–51. Cambridge, Mass., 1960.

Dray, W. H. "On the Nature and Role of Narrative in Historiography," *History and Theory* 10 (1971), 153–171.

Egermann, F. "Das Geschichtswerk des Herodot: Sein Plan," *Neue Jahrbücher für Antike und deutsche Bildung* 1 (1938), 191–197, 239–254.

Erbse, H. "Tradition und Form in Werke Herodots," *Gymnasion* 68 (1961), 239–257.

Fenik, B. *Typical Battle Scenes in the Iliad.* (*Hermes* Einzelschr. 21.) 1968.

Finley, M. I. "Myth, Memory and History," in *The Use and Abuse of History*, pp. 11–33. New York, 1975.

Finnegan, R. "A Note on Oral Tradition and Historical Evidence," *History and Theory* 9 (1970), 195–201.

—— "What Is Oral Literature Anyway?" in *Oral Literature and the Formula*, ed. B. A. Stolz and R. S. Shannon, pp. 127–176. Ann Arbor, Mich., 1976.

Fornara, C. W. *Herodotus: An Interpretative Essay.* Oxford, 1971.

Fränkel, H. "Eine Stileigenheit der frühgriechischen Literatur," in *Wege und Formen frühgriechischen Denkens*, pp. 40–96. Munich, 1960.

Gardiner, Patrick. *The Nature of Historical Explanation*. Oxford, 1952.

Gomme, A. W. *Essays in Greek History and Literature*. Oxford, 1937.

Goody, Jack. *The Domestication of the Savage Mind*. Cambridge, 1977.

Goody, Jack, and Watt, I. P. "The Consequences of Literacy," *Comparative Studies in Society and History* 5 (1963), 304–345.

Groningen, B. A. van. *La composition littéraire archaïque grecque*. Amsterdam, 1958.

Havelock, Eric A. "Prologue to Greek Literacy," in *Lectures in Memory of Louise Taft Semple*, 2d ser. Cincinnati, 1971.

Heni, R. *Die Gespräche bei Herodot*. Heilbronn, 1977.

Hohti, Paavo. *The Interrelation of Speech and Action in the Histories of Herodotus*. (*Commentationes Humanorum Litterarum* 57.) Helsinki, 1976.

Immerwahr, H. R. "Aspects of Historical Causation in Herodotus," *Transactions of the American Philological Association* 87 (1956), 241–280.

―――― *Form and Thought in Herodotus*. (American Philological Association Monograph 23.) Cleveland, 1966.

―――― "Historical Action in Herodotus," *Transactions of the American Philoloqical Association* 85 (1954) 14–45.

―――― "The Samian Stories of Herodotus," *Classical Journal* 52 (1956/57), 312–322.

Jacoby, F. "Herodotos" in *Realencyclopädie* Supplementband 2 (Stuttgart, 1913), 205–520.

Kazazis, J. N. *Herodotus' Stories and History: a Proppian Analysis of his Narrative Technique*. (Ph.D. dissertation, University of Illinois, 1978. University Microfilms, Ann Arbor, Mich., 1979.

Kennedy, G. A. *The Art of Persuasion in Greece*. Princeton, 1963.

Lattimore, R. "The Composition of the *History* of Herodotus, *Classical Philology* 53 (1958), 9–21.

Lohmann, D. *Die Komposition der Reden in der Ilias*. (*Untersuchungen zur antiken Literatur und Geschichte* 6.) Berlin, 1970.

Louch, A. "History as Narrative," *History and Theory* 8 (1969), 54–70.

Mandelbaum, M. "A Note on History as Narrative," *History and Theory* 6 (1967), 413–419.

Marg, W., ed. *Herodot: Eine Auswahl aus der neueren Forschung*. Munich, 1962.

Munz, P. "History and Myth," *Philosophical Quarterly* 6 (1956), 1–16.

Myres, J. L. *Herodotus, Father of History*. (Oxford, 1953).

Pohlenz, M. *Herodot, der erste Geschichtsschreiber des Abendlandes*. (Leipzig, 1937).

Porter, D. H. "History as Process," *History and Theory* 14 (1975), 297–313.

Regenbogen, O. "Herodot und sein Werk: Ein Versuch." *Die Antike* 6 (1930), 202–248.

Robertson, John C. *The Gorgianic Figures in Early Greek Prose*. Baltimore, 1893.

Romilly, J. de. "La vengeance comme explication historique dans l'oeuvre d'Herodote," *Revue des Etudes Grecques* 134 (1971), 314–337.

Scholes, Robert, and Kellogg, Robert. *The Nature of Narrative*. Oxford, 1966.

Schulz, Erwin. *Die Reden in Herodot*. Greifswald, 1933.

Solmsen, L. "Speeches in Herodotus' Account of the Ionian Revolt," *American Journal of Philology* 64 (1943), 194–207.

—— "Speeches in Herodotus' Account of the Battle of Plataea," *Classical Philology* 39 (1944), 241–253.

Stahl, H.-P. "Learning through Suffering," *Yale Classical Studies* 24 (1975), 1–36.

Starr, Chester. *The Awakening of the Greek Historical Spirit.* New York, 1968.

von Fritz, Kurt. *Die Griechische Geschichtsschreibung.* Berlin, 1967.

Waters, K. H. "The Purpose of Dramatization in Herodotus," *Historia* 15 (1966), 157–171.

White, Hayden V. "Historicism, History, and the Figurative Imagination," *History and Theory Beiheft* 14, 48–67.

—— *Tropics of Discourse: Essays in Cultural Criticism.* Baltimore, 1978.

Wood, Henry. *The Histories of Herodotus: An Analysis of the Formal Structure.* The Hague. 1972.

Index of Herodotean Speeches

Key to speech patterns

S – Single	Hex – Hexad
Pa – Pair	Hep – Heptad
Tr – Triad	Oct – Octad
Te – Tetrad	Ennead
Pe – Pentad	Decad
	Decahexad

Key to functions

M or m   – Motivating
E or e   – Explaining
P or p   – Pre-figuring
ME or me – mixed motivating and explaining

An upper-case letter indicates that the single speech and at least one of the pair are quoted directly; a lower-case letter indicates that the single speech and both speeches of the pair are indirectly quoted. Only singles and pairs are categorized by function; triads, tetrads, etc., have more complex functions and so are simply categorized by the nature of the individual speeches.

Key to nature

Q – Question   C – Challenge   S – Synthesis, Conclusion
A – Answer   R – Response   I – Information

Upper-case letters indicate that the speech is directly quoted; lower-case letters indicate that the speech is indirectly quoted. Parentheses around the letter indicate that the speech is reported as having been made, but it is not even indirectly quoted. Slashes are used in a few cases to mark off dependent units.

Index of Other
Herodotean Passages

Index of Homeric
Speeches and Passages

Martin Classical Lectures